INTENTIONALITY

The Secrets to Thriving at All Times

Radido Shadrack

Intentionality

Copyright © 2021 by Radido Shadrack

Tel: +254 721 405 827

ISBN: 9798405987118

Published By

House of Wealth Publishers

+254 737 405 827

houseofwealthpublishers@gmail.com

Table of Contents

Chapter Five

Chapter Six

Chapter Seven

Dedication

To the individual who finds life empty, aimless, busy, but not effective, may the writings of this book shine a light to the inner you and help you discover your sense of purpose and enable you to become Intentional in building your capacity for fulfilling your life's mission.

To the resilient human spirit with a desire to achieve something meaningful in life, may the pages of this book guide you to becoming intentional with your thoughts and actions.

To everyone who desires to become intentional with whatever they do, may this book add value to their lives.

Acknowledgement

Every accomplishment in life is the result of the Intentional efforts of others. Just like it takes a village to raise a child, it also takes a team to author a book. Being aware that we are the sum total of all the encouragements, criticism, mentorship, training, knowledge, and words of wisdom of many individuals whom we are privileged to instinctively connect with them, no one can therefore claim full credit of any measure of success in any endeavor. This final book you are studying is no different.

I want to first of all thank the CEO of creation, the almighty God who is an Intentional creator. There is nothing He created and deposited on planet earth that was not supposed to be, also there is nothing He did not create which was supposed to be created. You are the founder of the concept of Intentionality; for it is from you that we draw the instinct to do things intentionally. I will always adore and praise you for enabling me to discover my area of gifting at an early stage in life and for always leading me intentionally on the path to take.

Second, I want to thank the most precious person in my life, my beautiful beloved wife, my life's partner and the co-partner of our ventures Millicent M Radido, who allowed me the personal time to sit down for hours to Intentionally meditate and craft the foundation message of this book, sometimes late in the night at our study room, crafting words and shaping them patiently and skillfully into sentences, paragraphs, chapters, pages and ultimately into a life-transforming book you are currently studying. I am thankful to God for bringing you into my life at the very moment that I needed a helper. You are a great pillar of strength and support in my life.

I want also to sincerely thank the AMG Realtors Ltd team through their CEO Mr. Andrew Muthee for granting us an opportunity to engage and train their team of staff members for a couple of days for it was from engaging them that the idea, concept, and desire for writing this book was birthed. I would like to sincerely thank you very much for providing us with a mental breeding ground that led to the testing of principles written here and the birthing of this book. We are so much honored and humbled.

Last but not least, I would like to thank my spiritual father Bishop Dr. Mark Kariuki, and the entire team of Deliverance Church (HOB) pastors and members where my wife and I fellowship receiving spiritual nourishment and counsel. We are grateful for your continued prayers, moral support, and belief in us.

Intentionality

Lastly, to you our local and international clients both corporate companies that we have been privileged to train and consult with through Zionpearl Business Consultants Ltd and the readers who study our books, we are humbled for through you we can bring to life the messages we are privileged to pen in our books when you Intentionally execute the principles shared in them. May the message shared in this book enable you to succeed at all times.

Author's Foreword

This book that you're now holding in your hand and all of the writings it contains was once a formless idea residing at the back of my mind. The Intentionality book was intended into the material world by applying all of the principles written here. I managed to make my vibrational energy match up to the all creating source and allowed these words and ideas to flow through me directly to you, my reader. You're holding in your hands' evidence that anything we conceive in our minds we can achieve through intentional execution.

I, therefore, hand over to you the challenge of Intentionality in that, with all the ideas, opportunities, skills, energy and the perfect conducive environment God has given to you, purpose to intentionally take action and release your genius and your gift into our generation and contribute to the forward transformation agenda of the society. Let this book, therefore, teach you the benefits of being intentional and why it matters, let the message drafted in the pages of this book guide you on how to become intentional and finally let the book challenge, inspire and inform you about the field of intentionality for that is where true success and progress lies all the time.

Praises for the Book

Success and failure depend on your Intentions. When you intend to do something, you will succeed in it. The wisdom captured in this book can take you decades down the line. It is a book all dreamers, entrepreneurs, career people, business people, students & all those who want to attain massive success must intentionally commit and purpose to secure their copies. The book is an inspirational manuscript on how to master the secrets to thriving at all times just as the title suggests. Every leader who aspires to intentionally grow their business, make their career soar, or succeed in life must be ready to study this great book.

The Writer has dealt, trained, mentored & coached many people in Africa, and therefore the wisdom in this book is a golden gift for those who have never had a one on one with the author, trainer, and publisher Radido Shadrack. I highly recommend this book to you

George Wachiuri - CEO *Optiven group, Chairman Optiven Foundation, Author, Entrepreneur & philanthropist*

I am pleased with the opportunity and honor to offer my thoughts and raving review of this powerful book titled "Intentionality" by Shadrack Radido. This book brings to mind one of the focuses I have interpreted as "Thriving in difficulty times "With many of us NOW living during the COVID 19 pandemic. This book could not have come at a more appropriate time as we try to comprehend and cope with dynamic change in the way we live and interact.

This book offers tips and strengthens our ability to manage change. It offers us hope and strategies for managing challenges and thriving despite global health pandemic, financial catastrophes, and social difficulties. The SECRETS of Thriving at All Times is an important tool for leaders, business persons, and professionals in all disciplines among others. I find the teachings, skills, and strategies presented in "INTENTIONALITY" as a valuable tool in ensuring we succeed against all ODDs.

I congratulate Shadrack Radido the author, for his foresight, wisdom, and intellect which is well illustrated in his writing - As I have always said that WISDOM is the timely and effective Application of Knowledge and Experience. This book is resourceful and we must apply the skills and materials presented here deliberately, intentionally, and TIMELY.

Peter K Wairegi - *Executive Director & Chairman KPRA, Author, Business Coach & Lecturer at KCA University.*

The strategies that Radido Shadrack lays out in this book will help you to put the right amount of attention on where you place your intention. The Intentionality approach will ensure that you are consistent and persistent as you pursue your potential, whether in business or life.

David Meltzer - *Co-founder of Sports 1 Marketing, best-selling author, and top business coach*

"The Voice of reason is subtle, but often persistent and consistent. Radido is the embodiment of that fact, and this book is simply an extension of that Voice, with each of its paragraphs being applicable to all ages and races. It has to be intentional for it to be exceptional, Savour it."

Vincent Ouma, *Kenyan WASH Specialist*

This book titled Intentionality by Author Shadrack Radido is a must-read for moral and innovative leaders both locally and internationally. Intentionality is the inner engine that drives innovative leaders to tap the wellspring of their innate human creativity to address even the most intractable social problems. Intentionality makes us forward-looking, out-of-the-box and possibly driven.

I recommend this book for any moral and innovative leader who would like to utilize their God-given creativity to make advances and transformation in every sector of the human endeavor to challenge obstacles and search out new solutions.

Daniel Juma Omondi - *Executive Director - Global Peace Foundation Kenya*

This book contains rare gem that will equip you with the wisdom of getting things done when you commit to becoming Intentional with whatever you set your mind to do. Success or failure depends on being Intentional; even our God is an Intentional God. In fact, he is the CEO and founder of the concept of Intentionality! I therefore strongly recommend this book to everyone who is keen to thriving at all times.

Bishop, Dr. Mark Kariuki - *Presiding Bishop, and General Overseer Deliverance Church International*

Introduction:

Why Study this Book

"Once you learn to read, you will be free forever" ~ Fredrick Douglass

I learned an important lesson many years ago: "Always look carefully for someone's motivations and agenda." For example, whenever you read a book, ask yourself, *"Why did this person spend months or years crafting this material?"* and *"What is their agenda?"* *"What message does this book have that the author wanted to pass across to us?"* Sometimes the agenda is stated; other times, it's hidden in the writings of the author, but there is always an agenda. In this book, you don't need to look for a hidden agenda. I am glad to spare your time and inform you now the reason for putting together this book. The inspiration behind the writing of this book is to challenge you to become Intentional with what you think of and what you do; because *success is Intentional; and so is a failure.*

Since you have willingly picked this book for studying, there are high chances you want to make something significant out of your life. The message in this book is designed to exactly enable you to achieve that. All you need to do with this book is to strive and understand a few simple but core concepts of Intentionality that will change the way you think about yourself, your business, and all that you endeavor to achieve.

Success is Intentional and so is a failure, therefore through this book, you are going to gain deeper insights about Intentionality, why we should be intentional all times but above all, you will be inspired, challenged and equipped with practical wisdom, secrets to enable you to build an Intentional life, career, and business.

Remember this, that:

Not everything in this book is going to benefit you.

I know this may sound insensitive, but it's the truth. There is just a statement, a paragraph, or a chapter in this book that is designed to be an eye and mind opener to you, but you have to study the book to come across it. One of the beautiful things about learning any subject is the fact that you don't need to know everything, all you may need is to understand a few cores and critical concepts in the book that provides the most valuable lessons hence you build a body of knowledge and gain a deeper understanding as you apply those concepts and principles.

How To Maximally Make Use of This Book

I want you to understand that the purpose of a book is not only to inform but to contribute towards the transformation of your life and until a book has contributed to the transformation of your life, that book has not yet accomplished its purpose hence you are not yet done with it. Therefore, do not let the writing of this book gather dust in your bookshelf before it contributes towards the transformation of your life.

The concepts in this book are too profound to be absorbed by casual browsing or gulping down the whole book in one reading. Like I had written in my previous books, this book should be studied slowly and carefully, one chapter at a time, never rush on to the next page until you are sure you have understood the core concepts of Intentionality penned in this book and you are ready to implement them in your life, business and career.

All the successful and renowned influential people like Christopher Columbus, Benjamin Franklin, Abraham Lincoln, Thomas Edison, Henry Ford, Martin Luther King Jnr, Walt Disney, Mother Theresa, Bill Gates, Steve Jobs,

Colonel Sanders, Oprah Winfrey, and Barack Obama among others gained their influence because they had one thing in common. They were very intentional in what they were doing and the capacities they were building over the years.

Feel free therefore to use this as a workbook as you also build your capacity. Write marginal notes for yourself. Use a highlighter as you study and mark words or sentences or paragraphs or even inspiring quotes that seem vital and applicable to you. As you study this material, discuss the concepts in each chapter with your studying companion. In whichever way you choose to study this book, purpose to seek understanding and to intentionally apply the teachings shared in here to maximize everything written in the book.

I came across a mind-opening discovery and observation many years ago while in my primary school that I have been applying ever since. What I keenly observed is that the best-top performing students in the class were those who used to become the teacher once the teacher is done teaching a particular subject. By this, I mean that they used to teach us that which the teacher had taught, and by doing so they ended up retaining and understanding better the concepts that were taught.

The point I am trying to drive home is this, after studying this book, purpose to teach and explain to others the best lessons and concepts you've learned from this book to better both your and their lives. Do not just read this book, Intentionally Study it.

Preface

Everything begins from self hence it is important to intentionally develop self. It is vital to develop yourself because the value you develop in self is the value you will impact and transfer on others. You cannot give what you don't have; you cannot impact on others what you have not intentionally built in you. Finally, you cannot produce to your maximum profitability that which you have not intentionally developed inside you. So, the starting point of anything meaningful in life is when you intentionally develop it from within. The field of success has forever been desired by many, the young, the elderly, the poor, and the rich. All of them aspire to become persons of value and to achieve something significant before leaving planet earth. The question many have been asking is this.

Is success for the selected few? Or can anyone achieve and become successful?

Throughout our discussion in this book, we are going to address this issue and come up with simple and practical ways that you and I can commit religiously and follow intentionally so as to change our thinking and ultimately transform our lives as we achieve our various successes.

Chapter One

The Intentionality of Success

"Creation's gold mine is in you. The key to achieving it is a deliberate intention. Whatever your dream may be at this moment, identify it. If you cannot define your desire, it can never become your reality." Mary Manin Morrissey.

I was nervously shaking on my way to the first public speaking event in Nakuru County; during the journey, I was dreading to death. I was afraid that I could make a mistake or the audience would boo at me and or that I was too young and not yet ready to address that audience. I did not know what to do even though this is what I had desired and dreamt of doing. I didn't know how to introduce myself on stage, how to initiate a talk, break the ice, or even close or conclude my speaking. I remembered the past twelve months how I used to freely give to my colleague most of the speaking invitations that were coming my way because of fear and low self-esteem until one day a very special person in my life told me the reality of what I was doing, saying that if I continue with that habit of pushing aside opportunities that were coming my way, I would one day give away a breakthrough opportunity that I had been praying, preparing and waiting for. That statement was a wake-up call to me.

When I finally stood in front of the audience, I was sweating with anxiety. I stuttered through the first few minutes. I could barely recall what I wanted to say, my mind went black, I remember standing there; sharing a powerful story while simultaneously thinking on how the audience is thinking about my speech, diction, and appearance. Unfortunately, the same feeling came back again a few years later while I was writing my first book which took me five years of doubt on whether I was capable and qualified to write a book.

Fast-forward to this present day. I have spoken hundreds of times to various corporate organizations and I am privileged and humbled to have penned more than 4 books while working on my dream and goal of writing 200 books in my lifetime.

Something changed in my mind and life. Do you want to know what happened?

I committed to becoming Intentional with speaking, consulting, writing and publishing, and more so with facing what I was afraid of doing. After a short period, I had mastered what seemed difficult and scary at the beginning. I had conquered the fear in me.

Understanding Fear

"The absence of fear is not courage; the absence of fear is mental illness." **Po Bronson**

Fear can be explained as an unpleasant feeling one gets when he/she thinks is in danger. It is a natural response of our nervous system which was built in us for survival. However unnecessary fear can be generated in our nervous system and body from negative thoughts and imagined scenarios. Our fear generating system can't tell the difference between a real scenario and the one we imagine at the back of our mind. If you imagine a hurtful scenario your nervous system and body respond by creating fear as if the situation were real. If you have a mind that imagines negative thoughts, then a negative lifestyle is what your life will express since the external expression of something, represents the thoughts that expressed it.

Looking back at the early stages of my speaking and writing career, I could strongly relate to the Bible Story of how the Israelites were feeling when they were hard-pressed with Pharaoh and his powerful army while leaving Egypt since fear and doubt was clouding every path they were endeavoring to take.

From the Bible story of Moses and the children of Israel, there are several minds opening lessons about the phases of fear and how to overcome them that Rabbi Levi Brackman explained in simplicity from his book titled *Jewish wisdom for business success* that has been uplifting my spirit when I read it every time fear creeps in me.

From the day I understood those phases of fear, my life changed and these days *I am comfortable being uncomfortable in certain circumstances in my life.* Of the four phases of fear explained in that book, three of them strongly became part of my being. The three are; in the phase of fear, one is likely to retreat, fight, or move forward.

Imagine what it was like to be one of the Israelites gathered at the water's edge, with the hoofbeats of Pharaoh's cavalry booming in the near distance. The exultation of freedom is gone; you glance and in one direction there is the endless raging water while on the other direction you are staring at the looming war horses. You can hear the war-whoops of the charioteers. You look upwards at the sky, wishing you had wings, and wonder to yourself whether this is your last chance to gaze at the clouds drifting in the sky. The dust from the approaching army starts to cloud the air around you. You look into the eyes of your children and you feel their fear in your bones.[1]

As Pharaoh approached, the Israelites looked up, and there were the Egyptians, marching after them. They were terrified and cried out to the LORD. They said to Moses, "Was it because there were no graves in Egypt that you brought us to the desert to die? What have you done to us by bringing us out of Egypt? Didn't we say to you in Egypt, 'Leave us alone; let us serve the Egyptians'? It would have been better for us to serve the Egyptians than to die in the desert!" **Exodus 14:10**

If I was there at that particular time, I do not know how I could have reacted or responded; bearing in mind that pharaoh and his powerful army were just a distance away and on the other side the raging sea. Moses did not even try to argue with the people because he could feel their fear. Among the three phases of fear observed from the Israelites were:

---

1 Jewish wisdom for business success, accessed 19th February 2021

1. Retreat/Surrendering/ Throwing In The Towel

In times of crisis throwing in the towel than journeying ahead usually seems like the best option. According to the Israelites at that time, the thought of surrendering and going back into their former lives of slavery than to drown in the sea was the only solution most of them probably thought about.

They knew they could remain alive in Egypt however miserable their lives were. They knew that, despite anything else, life could still go on while in Egypt. Even though they had come farther than any of them could have imagined, the concept of backtracking must have sounded pretty appealing. Moses clearly understood this and did not try to shame them.

Instead, he gathered the courage, strengthened himself in the Lord, faced the people and acknowledged the situation as it was, and painted a brighter picture of hope to give them a reason to choose a different path.

Exodus 14:13 *"Though you see the Egyptians now, you will never see them again,"* he said. Such is usually the situation in our lives most of the time when we are faced with a temporary condition that might seem impossible to us at that particular time. Like I had mentioned earlier, when I went to my first public speaking event, the thought of quitting and throwing in the towel was so strong at the back of my mind that it clouded my ability to see breakthrough at the end of the tunnel. If I had thrown in the towel, right now you could not be reading this book nor be impacted with any of the projects we have been privileged to unleash.

2. Fight Back

When we are particularly fearful of an adversary, fighting back is often the most satisfying option. Remember that moment when you fought back a client with many defending words after telling you how poor your products or customer service was? Never fight your customers when they are giving you feedback whether positive or negative.

Since the Israelites were too terrified and defensive, the desire to try and battle the Egyptians was an understandable and even commendable reaction to the fear they felt towards them. However, in this case, God was their warrior. As quoted in **Exodus 14:13** Moses just told them. *"Stand firm and see the salvation that God will bring about today. Though you see the Egyptians now, you will never see them again. God will fight for you and you shall remain silent."*

God knew if the Israelites were to fight by themselves, they will need to turn and aim their attention backward; the goal though was to get home, not to retrace their steps and get into a fight. In my public speaking context even though there was no real enemy I was fighting; I believe the enemy I was fighting was within me. I was fighting the doubts that crowded within me which I had more often allowed them to triumph since I had so much doubt to the point of giving away opportunities that kept coming my way and passing them freely to another person.

3. Move On with Your Journey!

"If you can't fly then run, if you can't run then walk, if you can't walk then crawl, but whatever you do keep moving forward."

Moses commanded the Israelites to *"Move on"* as he was also commanded by God. Even though it was a simple and straight forward command I believe the fear that crippled the Israelites whispered to them that it wasn't a good idea to move forward into the water. The voice of their instincts told them they would surely drown. In boldness the Israelites did a miraculous thing: *they conquered their fear.* They chose to move forward. They chose to go into the uncharted territory, lifting their feet and journeying forward one step at a time rather than going back to what was familiar.

With a well-founded faith in God and in Moses, both of whom had proved to be trustworthy in the past, they walked straight into the water. As frightening as those first steps must have been, they overcame the paralysis that had come upon them; they intentionally raised their feet and placed them into the water. We all know what happened next; *a miracle occurred and the sea split.*

Just like how the Israelites gave us some timeless model of overcoming fear, you and I also need to deeply understand these blueprints and put them into practice whenever we are in a difficult situation clouded by fear and not knowing what to do. The wisdom of overcoming fear is therefore not in running away from the situation but in gathering the courage to move on with your journey despite being afraid.

I remember when I was up there on the stage, despite my body shaking and losing my speech, I never gave up, despite my mind going blank and running out of content several times when I was working on my book projects including this one, I never gave up. I kept on pushing on one paragraph at a time, one chapter at a time, and ultimately compiled a whole book and published it; to me, this is a great miracle that I do not take it for granted.

"You don't have to be great so you can start, but you need to start to become great." ~ Zig Ziglar

BENEFITS OF FEAR

Below are some of the benefits one can draw from a state of fear

1. Fear Helps to Heighten Our Awareness

At the basic level, fear guides our fight, flight, or forward movement responses and helps keep us safe and alive. Fear also heightens our senses and awareness; it keeps one in a state of alertness and helps in better preparation. The negative side of fear is when it holds one back from totally doing something positive.[2]

2. Overcoming Our Fears Help Others Overcome Theirs

When we have successfully learned how to deal with and overcome our fear, we can take an extra step to help others who are faced with the same. We can share our stories

---

2 Dancun Muguki: https://www.thriveyard.com/the-positive-side-of-fear-15-benefits-of-fear/ accessed February 2021

of how we overcame fear and share the strategies that we used to endure through our fears as I am doing through this book. Most of all, by sharing how we felt after we accomplished what we set out to do despite the fear, we can encourage and inspire other people to take action. Through my story and journey of book writing, many have been inspired to use the formula I devised on how to break down the concept of writing a book with ease.

"If you are not making someone else's life better, then you're wasting your time. Your life will become better by making other lives better." ~ Will Smith

3. Fear Helps One to Replicate the Breakthroughs

I realized from my own experience that the first time someone prevails over fear is usually the hardest. The second, third, or fourth time of facing the same fear becomes easier and easier. When I conquered the fear of writing the first book, I gathered the courage and writing became easy and fun to me, now this is my fifth book and with others in the pipeline to be released soon. When you have faced fear and taken steps to overcome that fear, the next time you face similar fears you can overcome them by recapping the steps that worked for you in the past.

It is beneficial to also keep making small intentional improvements in your process of mastering fear to make it better and better. Over time the steps for conquering fear can be ingrained on your mind to the point where you can face fear without it holding you back. Besides, other people have also faced fear and learned to bring it under control. To avoid mastering fear by trial and error, you can save time by talking to, reading, and learning about how others have succeeded in dealing with the fear that you are facing and then replicate their breakthroughs.

"I always think part of success is being able to replicate results, taking what is interesting or viable about yourself as a professional person, and seeing if you bring it into different situations with similar results." Robert Downey, Jr.

4. Fear Can Motivate Someone to Build Skills

Sometimes fear can point out the inadequacy that we have or what tools, skills, knowledge, or abilities we lack to progress on a desired course of action. It is fear that enabled me to hone my book publishing skills and now we are privileged to establish and run a publishing firm. Fear acts as an alarm clock reminding us that we need to do a bit more homework to pass the exam.

In this case, one can analyze what shortcomings are holding them back and take the necessary steps to mitigate those shortcomings such as learning new skills and widening one's knowledge.

"Take a limitation and turn it into an opportunity, take an opportunity and turn it into an adventure by dreaming BIG!" ~Jo Franz

5. Fear Helps to Activate Championship Mentality

How far did you go the last time when you faced fear and proceeded anyway? How much further can you go this time round? Turn your fears into a personal competition where you set a target for yourself and seek to break your record over and over again. Compete with yourself!

Assess what goals and targets you have set for yourself in the past, take stock of what you have achieved, and note the areas you have fallen short. Set bigger goals for yourself, stretch yourself, a breakout from the comfort zone, overcome the fear of failure, trying and trying again, and get back up when you fall. Learn from your own mistakes and those of others and take one step at a time as you move forward.

"All successful people men and women are big dreamers. They imagine what their future could be, ideal in every respect, and then they work every day toward their distant vision, that goal or purpose." ~ Brian Tracy

6. Fear Can Enable One to Identify Opportunities and Resources

Fear tells you that something could be missing. What resources do I have and what don't I have? It makes you realize that you don't have all the answers. Personally, through public speaking, fear enabled me to realize that I needed to practically engage myself with more speaking opportunities so that the fear of addressing masses in public can disappear. At the same time, it is humbling to know that you don't have all the answers and this encourages, cautions, and guides our progress to take steps such as learning from others and learning by yourself.

Get outside yourself and view yourself like an outsider – how would you advise yourself? How would you improve yourself? As a consultant to yourself, what suggestions and recommendations would you make to yourself? In the process of mitigating fear, one can also discover unexpected opportunities, solutions, and breakthroughs that they had not previously thought of or considered.

"Life hands us a lot of hard choices, and other people can help us more than we might realize. We often think we should make important decisions using just our internal resources. What are the pros and cons? What does my gut tell me? But often we have friends and family who know us in ways we don't know ourselves." ~ Sheena Iyenga

7. Fear Can Make One Break Routine

The presence of fear when undertaking a big goal tells you are stretching yourself and getting out of your comfort zone. The main worry would be; can I do this? The fear can stem from not being sure about how to do things. You wonder if your preferred mode of operation would work.

Should you do things the same way? Is there a better way to do it? What made you successful in the past may not necessarily make you successful in the future. Breaking the routine, therefore, involves re-imagining things and processes, identifying new patterns and possibilities to aspiring for, taking risks, exploring, and being adventurous with the ideas that might be coming your way hence succeeding when you act on them.

"If you expect life to be easy, challenges will seem difficult to you. If you accept that challenges may occur, life will be easier." ~ Rob Liano

8. Fear Enables Adequate Preparation and Planning to Take Place

Fear highlights the distance between where you are now and the goal to be achieved. Preparation, in this case, includes feeding yourself with positive messages, reading about others who have accomplished their goals, and allowing their experiences to be a source of motivation to you, imagining yourself as having achieved the goal and letting this mental imagery spur you onward.

Planning on the other hand includes documenting your starting point, seeing the big picture, breaking it down into smaller tasks, taking intentional action, and tracking your progress as you reach each small milestone. See beyond your current circumstances, envision where you want to be. A dose of perseverance helps one to stay in the game when you feel you don't have the energy to commit. It helps one to hang in there, to live to fight another day.

"If you don't know where you are going, you'll end up someplace else." **Yogi Berra**

9. Fear Inspires Intense Focus And Concentration

What do you want to achieve in life? Make a clear definition of your ultimate vision and success and back-it with the hunger to want to succeed. It is fear that inspired me to master the art of publishing books leading to the birth of the

House of Wealth Publishers. Therefore; come up with goals that will set you up for success and keep you in a trajectory where you can run consistently and have the confidence to jump over obstacles on your path, including fear.

Have the will to breakout, transcend, and rise above fear. When you are at the end of the rope and have to make do or die decisions, fear inspires intense focus. Fear keeps you alert, it keeps you surviving and progressing, it is a thermometer that let you know you are moving into a hot area and doing something beyond the normal.[3]

"If you are busy focusing on the falling bricks, you will never realize that they are truly stepping stones you need to cross over to the next phase of your life." ~ Kemi Sogunle

No Human Is Limited

The name Roger Bannister may not be familiar to you in this era unless you're a track and field fan, or historian of athletics. But the name Eliud Kipchoge of INEOS 1:59 challenge might be quite familiar. For those who don't know him, in 1954 Roger Bannister was the first man to break the four-minute barrier for the mile, which was a long-standing threshold that people had flirted with constantly but had never crossed.

Eliud Kipchoge on the other hand is the man who was able to run and complete a 42 km race in less than two hours and to be precise he covered the distance in 1:59 minutes which many couldn't fathom its possibility and believe it could not be done.

3 Dancun Muguki: https://www.thriveyard.com/the-positive-side-of-fear-15-benefits of-fear/ accessed February 2021

For Roger Bannister, one complete mile is four laps around a standard track. This means to break the four-minute threshold, a runner would need a pace of, at most, 60-seconds per lap; something that was thought to be impossible at that time also. The whole idea that a human being could run a mile in under four minutes was thought fantastic and even track experts predicted that humans would never do it. The world record for the mile was stalled around 4:02 and 4:01 for over a decade, so there seemed to be some truth to the belief that humans had finally reached their physical potential. Of course, similar notions of limits of human capabilities had existed, such as the 10-second barrier for the 100-meter dash.

At the 1952 Helsinki Summer Olympics, Bannister finished in fourth place in the 1500-meter run (the *metric* mile), just short of receiving a medal. Invigorated by his disappointment, he set his sights on running a sub-four-minute mile, which he felt would exonerate him. Bannister, unlike all other runners and experts at the time, believed that it was possible, so he trained with that in mind. It was a matter of *when* not *if* for him. All the while a doctor-in-training, Bannister began in earnest to attempt breaking the threshold in 1954. He accomplished the feat on May 6th. Such is also the case with Eliud Kipchoge who on 6 May 2017 on Autodromo Nazionale Monza in Milan, was the fastest participant and missed the two-hour target by 25 seconds.

With sheer focus, determination, continuous intentional practice on his daily routine exercises, he went ahead to break the two hours' record. Eliud Kipchoge said, *"I learned a lot from my previous attempt and I truly believe that I can go 26 seconds faster than I did in Monza two years ago. It gives me great pride to accept the challenge presented by INEOS. I am very excited about the months of good preparation to come and to show the world that when you focus on your goal, when you work hard and when you believe in yourself, anything is possible".* And on the 12th of October 2019, Eliud Kipchoge set the record of running 42 km in less than 2 hours.

Roger Bannister's achievement made people to be in disbelief and to revere as beyond human. For his efforts, he was knighted in 1975 and enjoyed a long life representing British athletic interests both domestically and internationally. But here's the shocking part of the story about Sir Roger Bannister and the four-minute mile. Within two months of his breaking the four-minute mark, an Australian runner named John Landy runners also broke the four-minute mark and since that time the four-minute mark has been broken many times by different athletes

Why did this happen? The effect of Intentionality took place.

Most people usually have preconceptions about what is possible and what is out of their reach. For some, this level of possibility can be high, and for others, it can be relatively low. Ultimately, the level of possibility is not important. It is the commitment of one to become intentional that matters. That's what drives us past a goal and when the going gets tough. In other words, when you are certain that something can be accomplished, and will be accomplished by you, you work in a tenacious way that allows it to happen.

In the months following Bannister's achievement, nothing about those other runners changed physically. They didn't magically grow winged feet or use performance-enhancing drugs as today's athletes do. They didn't alter their training habits or regimens. All that conceivably could have changed was their mindset, they were certain the four-minute threshold could be beaten, and they were going to do it! Knowing that something can be done has the potential of opening one's mind to the possibility of expecting success but your lack of becoming intentional is often your biggest obstacle to success. Such is the intentionality of success. *When you are intentional, most likely you will succeed.*

Intentionality

This Page was Intentionally Left blank

Chapter Two

Intend to Extend

What are Intentions?

"Our Intentions creates our reality" ~ Wayne Dyer

Intentions are the creative powers behind the change we see around us and the change one might desire in life. An intention is so powerful because it slowly shows people how incredibly powerful, they are. Every action we have as human beings starts with a thought, a desire, and an intention that sets its direction, path, speed, actions, consistency, and ultimately its outcome. Whether you want to write a book, quit your job, venture into consultancy, or set up charity work. It will need you to be Intentional. A decision fueled by the desire to make something happen.

Never underestimate the power of intention. Your thoughts, your words…they are keys to your future.

How Does the Concept of Intentionality Work?

The definition and explanation of what Intention is, is very easy to understand and explain, but someone might tend to wonder, what gives intentions power, and how do we get the most out of them? Like I have mentioned above, an intention starts with a mental picture of a change or goal you desire; whether material goal, spiritual goal, physical goal, or mental change that you want it reflects in your life.

Then it will require laser focus and action to make your intentions turn into reality. Setting an intention is activating a part of the human receptivity. Suppose you were to go out on a particular day, and not have set any intention of where you are headed to or even what to do, then you're getting on a vehicle with no direction. This can be fatal because it will mean that you are allowing fate to happen to you, but if you know that you want to get somewhere, the power of becoming intentional is going to help you get there.[4]

People these days frequently ask me, "Radido, how come you can write and publish one book after another within a short period? Where do you get the time and the content to write all these books? Including the time for the corporate training, speaking and even running a publishing firm and among other things?" Mostly these questions are usually followed by intense interrogation about various techniques and endeavors that consumes my energies and time and how others can follow that same path and produce quality results in their fields of interest as well.

---

4 Carolyn Boyes, The Little Book of Intentional Living accessed June 2021

While I do not have a one-size-fits answer for all the questions, I love to respond to these questions because they help me stay on course and committed to pursuing my purpose.

I love entrepreneurship and I like to consider myself an entrepreneur. To me, business simply means exchange, I am saying this because, some are in the business of exchanging products in the society and they are rewarded with money, while some are exchanging services to get money and even in our current technological advancement era, we have those who are in business majoring in exchanging of creativity and innovation just to get the return in the form of money. And so, whatever you are or will be exchanging that is what will become business to you. My desire for business on the other hand and for pursuing success for myself did not just grow in me suddenly; the bug hit me while I was still schooling. I wanted to prove to myself that I can create something of value to exchange to better the lives of others and mine as well.

Mental Independence for Intentional Living

"Great Intentions become tragic action when delivered without careful thought." ~ Michael Dooley

Over more than ten years I have been researching and studying the subject of success and people who are successful for my benefit. I could spend hours at the Kenya National Library studying magazines, articles, watching documentaries and reading books authored by successful people just to find out how they ended up where they are.

Intentionality

I was thrilled by what I came across, initially I was searching specifically for the kind of ventures successful people do to acquire wealth but I ended up observing a different mindset, attitude, and spirit that they have. To them, it's not what you do that matters but the mindset and the thinking you have concerning what you do and how you do it.

The mental change and attitude that I got from researching about them made me commit to applying those lessons for myself and observe whether my life will change as well and, for sure after a long duration of religiously applying what I have been learning my mind and life began to change for the better.

First, it was an inner uplifting of my level of confidence and since both fear and confidence are contagious, I was infected with a new level of poise knowing that I too can succeed if I consistently pursue my heart's desires. The other thing that got amplified in me was the hunger for knowledge and the desire to act on the new knowledge I had acquired.

Success has a way of attracting it's like-minded, therefore if you desire to attract success in your life, just commit to feeding your mind intentionally with what successful people feed theirs with and in no time your mind will begin to generate positive and great ideas which when acted upon you will become successful and cause you to attract other successful people hence keeping company with them as you continue to build your mental capacity.

Intend To Extend

Since the time I began writing this book, I committed to staying Intentional at all times with this gift given to me by the creator. Many were the times I did not feel like writing but I had to. I had to create time to write even if it was late in the night and slowly by slowly the thoughts and ideas I wrote were turning into paragraphs, chapters, pages, and eventually a life-transforming book you are reading.

When you intend to do something which means, to purpose, to plan or to expect, there are high chances you will extend which means to expand, to spread out or to increase. Every successful person I know or studied about who turned out to have accumulated great wealth began from the point of aiming for something because they understood that success is Intentional.

At one-time Ted Turner founder of CNN as captured in his book titled Call Me Ted thought of an idea of establishing a 24-hours news channel. This brilliant, unique, and scary idea came to him during a time when not even a single television station had started the concept of a 24-hour news channel. It was in the late 1970s and most newscasts those days used to be aired between 6:00, 7:00, and 11:00 P.M. Turner in his book said that he used to arrive at his home around 8:00 pm and to get up early the following day he'd sleep at around 10:00 PM. On many occasions, he would get most of his news from newspapers and weekly magazines.

He said *"I usually came home around 8:00 and since I got up so early in the morning, I'd be asleep around 10:00. I wound up getting most of my news from newspapers and weekly magazines and I figured that my experience was not unique—there had to be other people whose work hours were not conducive to watching the evening news."* It was this kind of a busy schedule and possibility thinking that birthed CNN, a globally respected television network known these days for its dramatic live coverage of breaking news. Ted also said that "Just over ten years after launching and being ridiculed as "Chicken Noodle News," CNN had established itself as the most capable, trusted news outlet in the world that other media houses locally and globally would visit just to benchmark from."[5]

"Intentionality fuels the master's journey. Every master is a master of vision." ~ George Leonard

Ted Turner of CNN is not the only one known to have used this concept of intending to extend, the powerful concept of aiming with a purpose and staying committed at something until it bears fruits. The late Steve Jobs of Apple also brought a dent in the universe with computer products and Bill Gates also did the same with computer software, without also forgetting Jeff Bezos who did it with online ordering and delivering of products and services through Amazon. When you aim at something, committing without removing your focus from it, you will surely extend just like the above-mentioned persons of global influence did.

---

5 Ted Turner with Bill Burke-Call Me Ted, Page 158 accessed June 2021

Execution Planner Works Wonders

"Plan your work and work your plan."

One thing that never fails to amaze me is the power of writing things down. I am convinced there is some sort of miracle that happens in my brain when I write down my intentions in my execution planner because when I do, it's so much easier to follow them through than when I don't write. Like I had mentioned to you in my opening statement of this chapter about the numerous genuine questions I have been receiving lately concerning the effectiveness of the book writing projects I normally undertake. The answer to those many questions lie with a custom-made book dear to me called *The Execution Planner.*

I used to experience lots of challenges, especially with execution. Lots of Ideas would come to my mind but still, I could not benefit from any of them simply because I had not placed a premium on execution, and like I often say *"Ideas don't make you Rich. Execution of those ideas does."* I realized that for me to become effective with the art of execution, I had to be an Intentional planner of the things I wanted to pursue and include them in my do-to list every day.

You can even place an order to purchase a copy of the Personal Execution Planner Book I created through the email and contacts shared in this book and begin to become effective with what you do and with the ideas that come to your mind.

The personal execution planner I created has two sections. On the left side, there is a section where you record different activities in different time zones. When you wake up early in the morning, you begin by highlighting the different things you intend to do from early in the morning till late at night as indicated in the different time zones.

Capturing the daily activities in that manner helps one to approach a particular day intentionally thus achieving more compared to one who just wakes and begins to experience the day without a plan. The beauty of highlighting the things that you are intending to do is that it helps you to commit and become focused hence avoiding unnecessary distractions which most of the time tend to delay us from achieving our goals and targets. Also with this concept, one can plan his time effectively and schedule meetings and programs according to their priorities and return on time invested.

On the right side of the Execution Planner book is a journaling section. The beginning of a year usually marks the time of writing New Year resolutions, which from my keen observation from close friends and family by mid of the new month of the year, most people usually tend to tiptoe back to their previous routine of doing things thus failing to achieve what was in their set resolutions by the stipulated deadline.

This often happens when one draft down their New Year resolution goals and then shelves them away in a place where they cannot see and review them daily. As the English proverb goes *"Out of sight, out of mind"* With the Execution Planner and especially on the right side of it, you will be able to establish your goals daily. With the rising of the sun each day, it gives you an opportunity and a time to yet fulfill your daily goal which ultimately contributes towards the fulfillment of your annual goals and your year's resolution. On that side, there is a section where you begin with your daily goals, with this I mean you write the number of goals you are intending to fulfill on that particular day.

Once you are done with that, below it you will come up with the number of targets which you will derive from the goals you had written on top. For example, on a certain day, your goal might be to achieve 6 different things and out of the six, the target that you have set for yourself is just to fulfill 4 out of the 6. This way you will become effective when you commit to acting on your goals and targets.

The most brilliant part of the planner is the section below where in the evening after you have pursued and fulfilled your day's activities you will note down the activities you were able to accomplish on that particular day. Doing this will inspire you to yet again similarly face the following day with confidence thus mastering the art of execution.

Mastering the art of execution will therefore separate you from the masses, some of whom seem to be busy but not effective and so equipping yourself with a Personal Execution Planner every day will be a game-changer for you as it has been for me. This is the push that has given me the privilege to be writing and releasing books one after the other even though I feel I haven't gotten where I want to be yet.

Sample of the Execution Planner

Date: ....   **Execution Schedule**

5:30am-9:30am

....
....
....

9:30am-12:30pm

....
....
....

12:30 pm-3:30pm

....
....
....
....

3:30pm-6:30pm

....
....
....
....

6:30pm-9:30pm

....
....
....

9:30pm-Later

....
....
....

Write Goals   **Execution Journal**

....
....
....
....
....
....
....
....
....

Inspiring Quote of the day:

....
....
....
....

Targets:

....
....
....
....
....
....
....

Accomplishments of the day:

....
....
....
....
....
....
....
....
....
....
....

Seven Benefits of Intentionality

When you commit to purposefully set and work on your intentions, you will take responsibility for the outcome because you now know why you do what you do, and if it doesn't work, you can set a different intention. An Intentional person is no longer the victim of circumstance. Instead of letting the world decides for you, you become the author of your destiny and decide what you wish to create in your life.

What is ultimately important for most people is not accumulated possessions or accolades but the feeling of being in charge and ultimately in control of your life, that feeling of not being afraid of taking action and pushing your idea to produce results is what every one of us would want to have.

I am a proud student of the concept of Intentionality, after applying this concept religiously for years now, right from when I was an amateur in corporate training, business consulting, writing and publishing, I have truly benefited from this concept for it has made me to become a pro and to master the art of whatever I set in my mind to do.

Below are some of the benefits this concept will bring to you when you purpose to apply it.

1. When You Are Intentional You Become Purpose-Driven

The question of one's purpose and the search for the meaning of life has puzzled people for so long I included. I believe this is because we typically begin at the wrong point which is focusing on *ourselves*. Rick Warren in his book

Purpose Driven Life observed that we tend to ask self-centered questions like, what do I want to be in life? What should I do with my life? What are my goals, my ambitions, and dreams for my future? But focusing on ourselves will never reveal our life's purpose.

If you seek to truly understand the purpose of a thing, never ask the thing but the creator of that thing. A good example is this. If you want to know the purpose of a plane, never ask the plane but the manufacturer who came up with that plane. Likewise, for our case as human beings, it is our creator who truly knows the purpose and the reason as to why He created us. And so, find out from your creator and He will for sure let you know the Why for your living.

He Is Intentional

Our maker is an Intentional creator, I believe He didn't create and bring us into planet earth in vain, but He did so for us to fulfill a certain specific purpose. In the same way, the manufacturers of airplanes such as Learjet, Gulfstream, or Boeing among others did not just came up with those machines for the fun of it but to fulfill the air transportation agenda they had in mind and so, they had to be intentional while making them.

You must therefore begin with God your Creator to intentionally understand your purpose in life. We exist only because God wills that we do. We were made by God and for God and until we understand that life will never make sense to us, it will forever remain to be a chase after the wind. It is therefore only in God that we discover our origin, our identity, our meaning, our purpose, our significance, our destiny, and finally our Intentionality since every other path leads to a dead end[6].

Life is all about what your creator fashioned you to become, you should therefore endeavor to create time and talk to Him to find out the purpose and the reason for your existence. God is not just the starting point of your life; He is the source of it. To discover your purpose in life you must turn to God's word, not the world's wisdom. Since He is a faithful God, He will always answer your request, and when you get the answers to your request, purpose to become intentional with your thinking, action, and results; when you are Intentional, you will become purpose-driven. *Hence Intentionality breed's purpose.*

2. When You Are Intentional You Gain Mastery

Robert Greene in his book titled Mastery captured this concept so profoundly and in simplicity. Every time I am involved in a new project that I have never undertaken, the wisdom of this man guides me all the way, assuring me that if I continue to commit and to immerse myself intentionally to gaining knowledge of what I am doing I will eventually gain mastery hence be in charge. As I had captured Greene's wisdom in my previous book titled Execution he says:

"There exists a form of power and intelligence that represents the highest point of human potential. It is the source of the greatest achievements and discoveries in history. It is an intelligence that is not taught in our schools nor analyzed by professors, but almost all of us, at some point, have had glimpses

6 Rick Warren, Purpose Driven life page 18 accessed November 2021

of it in our own experience. It often comes to us in a period of tension facing a deadline, an urgent need to solve a problem, a crisis of sorts. Or it can come as the result of constant work on a project. In any event, pressed by circumstances, we feel unusually energized and focused. Our minds become completely absorbed in the task before us.

This intense concentration sparks all kinds of ideas that come to us as we fall asleep, out of nowhere, as if springing from our subconscious mind. At these times, other people seem less resistant to our influence; perhaps we are more attentive in them, or we appear to have a special power that inspires their respect. We might normally experience life in a passive mode, constantly reacting to this or that incident, but for these days or weeks, we feel like we can determine events and make things happen.

We could express this power in the following way: Most of the time we live inside a world of dreams, desires, and obsessive thoughts. But in this period of exceptional creativity, we are impelled by the need to get something done that has a practical effect. We force ourselves to step outside our inner chamber of habitual thoughts and connect to the world, to other people, and reality. Instead of flitting here and there in a state of perpetual distraction, our minds focus and penetrate to the core of something real.

Once the deadline has passed or the crisis is over, this feeling of power and heightened creativity generally fades away. We go back to our distracted state and the sense of control is gone. If only we could manufacture this feeling, or somehow keep it alive longer, but it seems so mysterious and elusive.

This feeling truly comes when one understands their Why for living and when they are Intentional in fulfilling it. The problem we face is that this form of power and intelligence is either ignored as a subject of study or is surrounded by all kinds of myths and misconceptions, all of which only adds to the mystery. We imagine that creativity and brilliance just appear out of nowhere, the fruit of natural talent, or perhaps of a good mood, or an alignment of the stars.

Let us call this sensation knowledge of thyself the feeling that we truly understand and that we are in control of our sense of purpose, the one thing we were born to pursue and fulfill. For some of us, mastering our field becomes our way of life, our way of seeing the world. The process can be illustrated in the following manner: Let us say we are learning the piano, or entering a new job where we must acquire certain skills. In the beginning, we are outsiders; our initial impressions of the piano or the work environment are based on prejudgments, and often contain an element of fear.

When we first study the piano, the keyboard looks rather intimidating, we don't understand the relationships between the keys, the chords, the pedals, and everything else that goes into creating music. In a new job situation, we are ignorant of the power relationships between people, the psychology of our boss, the rules and procedures that are considered critical for success. We are confused and the knowledge we need in both cases is over our heads.

Although we might enter these situations with excitement about what we can learn or do with our new skills, we quickly realize how much hard work there is ahead of us. The great danger is that we give in to feelings of boredom, impatience, fear, and confusion. We stop observing and learning and failing to become Intentional. The process comes to a halt. If, on the other hand, we manage these emotions and allow time to take its course, something remarkable begins to take shape.

As we continue to observe and follow the lead of others, we gain clarity, learning the rules and seeing how things work and fit together, if we keep practicing, we gain fluency; basic skills are mastered, allowing us to take on newer and more exciting challenges. We begin to see connections that were invisible to us before. We slowly gain confidence in our ability to solve problems or overcome weaknesses through sheer persistence.

At a certain point, we move from student to practitioner. We try out our ideas, gaining valuable feedback in the process. We use our expanding knowledge in increasingly creative ways. Instead of just learning how others do things, we bring our style, individuality, and taste into play, the Steve Jobs way or Henry Ford's way. As months go by and we remain faithful to this process, yet another leap takes place to gaining mastery.

The keyboard is no longer something outside of us; it is internalized and becomes part of our nervous system, our fingertips. In our career, we now have a feeling for the group dynamic, the current state of the business. We can apply this feeling to social situations, seeing deeper into other people and anticipating their reactions. We can make decisions that are rapid and highly creative. Ideas come to us. We have learned the rules so well that we can now be the ones to break or rewrite them.

Intentionality

In the process leading to this ultimate form of power, we can identify three distinct phases or levels. The first is the apprenticeship; the second is the Creative-Active; the third is Mastery. In the first phase, we stand outside of our field, learning as much as we can of the basic elements and rules. At this level, we have only a partial picture of the field and so our powers are limited.

In the second phase, through much practice and immersion, we have a glimpse of the inside of the machinery, how things connect with each another, and thus gain a more comprehensive understanding of the subject. With this, comes a new power, the ability to experiment and creatively play with the elements involved.

In the third phase, our degree of knowledge, experience, and focus is so deep that we can now see the whole picture with complete clarity. We have access to the heart of life to human nature and natural phenomena. That is why the artwork of masters touches us to the core; the artist has captured something of the essence of reality. That is why the brilliant scientist can uncover a new law of physics and the inventor or entrepreneur can hit upon something no one else has imagined, like Facebook, Twitter, Zoom, WhatsApp or Instagram and to the authors like us we can be at a state where we are releasing books one after the other within a short time, among other creative innovative ideas. All these could be happening simply because the individual allowed to be directed by purpose through being Intentional and mastering knowledge of thyself and becoming effective with execution.

We can call this power instinct; this flash of instinct is what ultimately brings us closer to reality, as our minds suddenly become illuminated by some particle of truth previously hidden to us and others. An animal can learn, but it largely relies on its instincts to connect to its surroundings and save itself from danger. Through instinct, it can act quickly and effectively, humans rely instead on intellect to understand their environment. But sometimes intellect can be slow, and in its slowness can become ineffective. Intuitive powers at the mastery level are a mixture of instinct and intellect. It is our way of making sudden and powerful connections to the environment.

If we move through the process to this endpoint, we activate the intuitive power latent in every human brain, one that is connected to your why for living and a sense of personal fulfillment and by doing so you become effective in the marketplace and with the creative product you are introducing into your field of influence and exchange.[7]" This, therefore, shows that when one commits to becoming Intentional he/she will gain mastery in whichever field of interest they choose to pursue, and thus Intentionality helps one to gain mastery.

3. When You Are Intentional You Become Committed

According to the explanation given in Merriam-webster dictionary, commitment is defined as a state or quality of being dedicated to a course, an activity, or an engagement until its results have been achieved. Malcolm Gladwell in his book titled Outliers talks about the concept of the 10,000-hour rule which he did research and observed that it takes at least 10,000 hours of Intentional practice and commitment

---

7 Robert Greene- Mastery page 1, accessed February 2021

to a particular course of action for one to gain mastery. Committing to staying focused therefore provides one with clarity, creativity, and definiteness of purpose. In which when you are Intentional you will find it easy to commit and to place a premium on execution.

4. When You Are Intentional You Get Things Done

Once again, the Wright brothers are a great example of a team that was so Intentional to the course they were pursuing until they succeeded. They taught us that intentionality leads one to become effective with execution. On the other hand, when you are Intentional, you activate the three levels of the human mind which are the conscious mind, the subconscious mind, and ultimately the body.

The Conscious Mind

In Homeless Money, I mentioned that the conscious mind is that part of the body that receives information and does the thinking job. It helps one to filter into his subconscious mind the thoughts that will be entertained or rejected.

When you intentionally allow thoughts to enter into your mind, they will be filtered into the subconscious mind and eventually processed and expressed out through the body in the form of results-oriented actions. Information enters the mind through this first level of entry. According to the deeper explanation I shared in that book, I said there are six strong mental muscles through which information enters in this first level of entry that makes the conscious mind becomes such a powerful tool that man has ever possessed.[8]

8 Millionaire-Mindset-Gerry-Robert, accessed February 2021

The Subconscious Mind

This is the most crucial part of the human mind; it is the zone that produces superiority when an individual masters his or her gifts. Every thought, idea, picture, or image fed and filtered by the conscious mind finds its ways into the subconscious mind. Whatever is transferred from the conscious to the subconscious mind gets processed and the outcome expressed out of one's life. The subconscious mind does not understand the message of *"can't"*, it simply absorbs the pictures and images fed into it by the conscious mind and then create an exact reality for them through the expression out of the body. Whatever information is impressed into the subconscious mind; will ultimately find expression through the body.

When you subject into your mind thoughts of not being Intentional with what you are doing or what you intend to do, the thoughts will be filtered into the subconscious mind and ultimately expressed out of your life. The human subconscious mind usually receives information as a command whose answers must be provided at all costs. When the thoughts of "I can't" come into your conscious mind, it will pick the thoughts and send them into the subconscious mind where they get worked on.

The Body

I said that the human body is the least and the smallest part of our entire body system, yet the most visible of them all. The body was designed to act according to the information intentionally fed in and that is why whatever the subconscious mind receives it must be expressed out through the body.

We should, therefore, endeavor to feed our minds intentionally with thoughts of possibilities and our body will have no choice but to yield those outcomes. The conscious, subconscious and the body plays a vital role in the story of execution because when one is not intentional getting things done will be next to impossible but when you are intentional you activate these levels of the mind and most likely you will place a premium on execution.

5. When You Are Intentional You Become Transformational

The evidence of human progress is usually transformation. You cannot claim progress in life yet there is no evidence of change on both the internal and external expression of your life. Transformation is the evidence of progress and change and for one to claim that he/she is transforming you ought to be Intentional in the transformation agenda. When I think of the word transformation,

I imagine a butterfly. Before the butterfly takes dominance into the sky displaying its beautiful colors it usually emerges from becoming a crawling caterpillar which was initially a dormant egg attached to a tree branch, when one becomes Intentional transformational change will be experienced.

6. When You Are Intentional You Become Influential

Intentionality breeds influence. Any person who commits to a particular cause of action over some time and gains mastery in the course eventually becomes a voice in that particular field and gains influence. Let's take an example of an athletic sport such as football or basketball. For more than 20 years Michael Jordan has been on the basketball courts practicing the game almost daily whether he felt like doing so or not, it was his commitment to hanging around the courts thar made him become a legend in the game. This insane Intentional commitment habit eventually paid off. MJ turned out to be very exceptional and influential in the world of basketball sport and athletics in general. This therefore proves that if you and I continue to building capacity in our various areas of interest, we will eventually command Influence.

7. When You Are Intentional You Become Exceptional

Exceptionality in life is a result of being Intentional with your thoughts, plans, and actions. Being exceptional means, you've already gained mastery in the things you had committed to pursuing and so you are an asset to be sought after in your particular field of operation. One of the beautiful things about being exceptional is that it makes you unique and extraordinary and this can position you to a platform where you can either command resources or the resources locate you easily and one of them being money. All gifted and exceptional individuals in the world in certain areas can easily attract resources.

This Page was Intentionally Left blank

Chapter Three

Intentionality: The Secret to Surviving and Thriving During Tough Times

"Tough times don't last, but tough people do" Robert Schuller

What do you do when everything you had put your trust in collapses?

How do you prepare for a sudden change in life?

How do you recover when life hits you hard?

After a lifetime of hard work, dedication, **commitment**, and loyalty to a chosen career, how do you suddenly change your vocation and skillsets especially when the COVID-19 pandemic hits you?

What do you do when a lifelong dream and investment is suddenly taken from you through no fault of your own?

How do you carry on after a business you had built from the grounds up for many years is swept by COVID-19 pandemic?

How do you bounce back after institutions that were expected to protect you suddenly pull the rugs out from under your life in the name of downsizing?

What do you say to your family when you face the reality that you may no longer be able to fulfill their expectations for security, support, and provision?

Where do you go when you want to work but there are no jobs and almost everyone has been ordered to work from home?

What do you do when your sense of pride for personal accomplishment is dashed in the stress of survival?

How do you go on after the legacy of years of work is erased by a crisis that has almost brought the entire world to a standstill?

Where do you go when the ones you go to for help are also in need of help?

What do you do when your leadership is faced with a crisis?

Is a crisis a good thing or does it come to destroy us?

As of the writing of this book the world is in a crisis, there is an outbreak of coronavirus from Wuhan in China popularly known COVID-19 that has claimed the lives of more than 400,000 people while millions of others have already been infected. While affected nations are in total lockdown, millions around the globe are in a panicking mode, canceling their flights, postponing their business meetings, I don't know until when.

Others restricting their travels and many airlines and hotel industries experiencing billion's worth of losses due to this tragic outbreak. *"Well, as you know, from 15 to 20 years ago China was already dubbed as 'the factory of the world' so then what we have seen now is that the supply chain sourcing has been interrupted,"* Reuben Mondejar, professor for Asian Initiatives at the IESE Business School, University of Navarra, tells Al Jazeera news concerning the COVID-19 outbreak in China.

The Intentional ones on the other hand are benefiting from the precious opportunities brought along by this crisis. I previously wrote that the Japanese interpret the word crisis as an opportunity since during a moment of crisis that is when those who are Intentional will come up with creative solutions to combat the crisis. The recent outbreak of COVID-19 caused panic buying in some areas which led to supermarkets seeing their shelves cleared of essentials such as food items, toiletries, hand sanitizers, facemasks among other items.

The companies that had strategically positioned themselves well in the marketplace are reaping great returns in leaps and bounds during this season. During a crisis, the champions who bring groundbreaking solutions are always remembered in the minds and hearts of the people as true heroes.

Chester Arthur, who served as President of the United States from 1881 to 1885, might not be remembered by many as one of America's great leaders. Many Americans would be hard-pressed to identify him as one of their presidents! Arthur, who served after President Garfield's assassination, may well have possessed the basic qualities of a great leader. However, the time of his presidency was fairly stable, so he was never called upon to step up.

What have I learned from President Garfield? *It's simple: tough times breed great leaders and great success.* The same case applies to running any business venture or planning something and crisis hits you. A crisis provides a breeding ground for the principles of Intentionality to be put into practice. I have heard that the Japanese are usually happy when a crisis occurs, because to them they have come to interpret the word crisis as an opportunity to provide a unique solution thus reaping from it.

The Chinese uses two brush strokes to write the word "crisis." One brush stroke stands for danger; the other for opportunity. In a crisis, be aware of the danger—but recognize the opportunity." John F. Kennedy

If you look at many of the famous leaders throughout history, you'll notice they became famous because they navigated through seemingly impossible tough times. They held the flashlight at the end of the tunnel. Legendary leaders such as Abraham Lincoln, Martin Luther King Jnr, Steve Jobs, Bob Collymore, Franklin Delano Roosevelt, and the former US president Barrack Obama among others come to mind. All historical public figures were faced with incredibly complex or catastrophic situations.

Instead of cowering in indecision, they reacted boldly and aggressively. They threw conventional wisdom out of the window and intentionally developed their playbooks on the spot. So, what does this have to do with entrepreneurs and more specifically, those with the desire to succeed? I've discovered that being successful is all about being Intentionally able to rise to the occasion during tough times. Almost every entrepreneur or business leader has been faced with several instances where the fight or flight thinking kicked in, and while it seems very hard to brave the difficulty, it's always important to Intentionally tackle the tough times head-on.

What do you do when sales and revenue are falling short? What do you do when your organization is facing the prospect of downsizing? What do you do when your best employee suddenly quits? What do you do when your family is infected with COVID-19? No matter the circumstances, your team's morale is at an all-time low, and it's your job as their leader to lift their spirits and get them back on track.

In such tough times, many organizations take draconian steps to *"survive,"* but these steps can become a cause of their ultimate demise. Conversely, great companies led by intentional and creative visionaries often shine in these times, because they buck the trend of doom and gloom, and succeed in making their operations even stronger and more relevant. When times are great, everyone's a hero but when times are tough, great leaders emerge. So, today's business climate can provide just the opportunity to become an even more effective and inspiring leader to stand out in the crowd.

During hard times, you need leaders who can see and speedily seize opportunities as they present themselves. Possessing leadership capabilities on the other hand does not necessarily have anything to do with a title but has everything to do with being intentional and to deliver effective results.

The leaders or entrepreneurs who will be most successful during hard times are those people in an organization who are intentional and have embraced the concept of Intentionality with everything they set out to do. Below are some key strategies that enable an Intentional leader to lead their teams to not only survive but thrive during tough economic times as deeply illustrated in Becoming Maverick by author John Thiong'o:

1. Intentionally Build Trust

Trust is the currency of business relationships. Trust-building is a particularly old golden nugget that has withstood the test of time. In tough times, great leaders aim at pulling together with their teams. The biggest scapegoat for failure at the workplace is a lack of collaboration and poor communication.[9] You must earn the trust of your people. Trust does not just come by; you have to intentionally build it over time through consistency and to some degree, vulnerability. Consistency doesn't mean being rigid, but rather you demonstrate steadfast character, reliability, and fairness.

2. Show Compassion

With trust as the bedrock of your relationship with your team, compassion is the humanizing attribute for your

9 John Thiong'o, Becoming Maverick, accessed February 2021

leadership during tough times. When times are bad, your team knows how to receive bad news. Inevitably, you have to deliver the bad news, when necessary, but more importantly, is to know how to deliver them effectively:

Seek to understand: Stephen Covey, the author of the famed book *"7 Habits of Highly Effective People,"* says that we seek first to understand. The best way to do so in the heat of the moment is to practice *"active listening."* Say less, ask more, and if you can paraphrase your partner's conversation back to them and get their acknowledgment that you have understood, you are already succeeding.

3. Intentionally Identify and Work on Your Why?

Intentional people tend to mostly ask *why* questions. You may think it goes without saying, but your clarity around *why* the question is critical for the success of your mission in the organization. *Why* does the organization exist? Why are our products and services needed in the market? What is the purpose of my position in the organization and what can I do to be a solution provider?

Clarity of purpose is vital to longevity. What unites the long-lasting organizations of the world, no matter where they operate? It is usually a sense of purpose, a mission, a calling, and the execution ability of each of the team players and contributors. To succeed in tough times, we must identify the reason as to why we are undertaking the journey in the first place. This is important because you are almost always guaranteed discomfort and setbacks when you set off in your pursuit of purpose.

4. Introduce Stability

The absence of stability could be an indication of a tough season or times. On the other hand, stability is something we don't often think about as a leadership quality until it is absent. During tough times the leader needs to prioritize stabilization of the organization.

You want your team to know that after all, tough times will not last! There is hope! Such leaders show composure despite the tough situation in the operating environment. The composure of a leader is reflected in their attitude, body language, and overall presence.

An intentional leader always has a true north: he/she displays a strong set of convictions while being capable of keeping an open mind. Great leaders display actions and thoughts that are in line with the organizational purpose and the core values that they uphold. This builds stability both for and within their team. When teams know the leader's true north, they follow with confidence despite the tough times.

5. Control Your Fear

An entrepreneur in the workplace is like a general in the army. As bullets whiz by him/her the easier and human thing is to be afraid and sometimes quit. However, a great leader realizes that they have to subdue fear because his soldiers (the employees and team members) are looking up to him/her for clues on how to react.

Courage doesn't mean the absence of fear, and of course, being a leader certainly doesn't mean charging ahead blindly in the face of adversity. It does mean you can't allow your fear to become contagious. Your team needs to believe you're in control of yourself if they're to have confidence that you can make smart decisions in tough times.

6. Strive To Be Unique

Does your organization provide unique solutions? During tough times, organizations that survive and excel are those that provide solutions that are exceptional and distinctive. In the rash to contain the COVID 19, research institutes and vaccine making organizations are rushing to coming up with suitable vaccines that can be used to control the virus outbreak.

Zoom, a videotelephony proprietary software program developed by Zoom Video Communications gained popularity during the COVID19 pandemic season enabling millions of people to continue with communication and keeping in touch virtually. The uniqueness of your brand will give it the much needed "noticing power."

Your organization should have an element that differentiates it from the competition by grabbing people's attention. For example, Safaricom's M-PESA has been very successful mainly because of its simplicity of use and reliability.

In the year 2019 Safaricom rebranded and adopted the tag-line SIMPLE, TRANSPARENT, HONEST. That simplicity has driven Safaricom's growth in Kenya to unimaginable heights. What makes you or your product unique that can enable your organization to survive during tough times?

7. Innovate To Succeed and To Survive

To innovate is to survive. If your organization is not seeking innovative ways of production or service delivery, then it's just a matter of time before competition wipes you out of the market.

Bill Gates in his book titled Business @ the Speed of thought said *"In three years every product my company makes will be obsolete. The only question is whether we'll make them obsolete or somebody else will.... One day somebody will catch us napping. One day an eager startup will put Microsoft out of business. I just hope its fifty years from now and not in two or five years to come"*[10]

One sure way to kill innovation is to stay in your corner, do your things, and avoid interacting with others. This self-isolation from others has been termed the *Silo Effect* by US anthropologist and finance journalist Gillian Tett. Take Sony for instance, once an electronics giant company. Sony had been innovative at first, but over the years, it grew complacent. Apple's release of the iPod sounded the death knell of the Walkman, and in desperation, Sony appointed the first non-Japanese CEO in history UK executive Howard Stringer-in 2005.

In his first address to the employees, Stringer said, *"Sony is a company with too many silos!"* and tried his best to get the people to communicate with one another. But it was too late. Silos were already entrenched, and people did not want to leave their comfort zone. According to Tett, Facebook is an example of an innovative company with few, or no, silos.

10 Bill Gates-Business @ the speed of thought, page 155 accessed February 2021

"Employees are rotated around projects, urged to switch teams, given new challenges. The corporate culture is reinforced with group activities and slogans printed on posters: Move fast, break things! Done is better than perfect! In meetings, you are not allowed to talk about 'those idiots in team six' or 'those stupid marketing guys'...Employees are people first, their job title second." Innovate, before it is too late. If your organization does not continue to innovate, it will soon fade away. The organizations that succeed focus on infusing newness into their signature products and services.

One of the things that we intentionally do at our company is to look at our business from different eyes. We internally look at ourselves through the eyes of competition and ask ourselves questions such as. If we were the competition, what would we do to put House of Wealth Publishers out of business? Doing this frequently has enabled us to become creative hence unleashing creative and innovative ideas and concepts throughout.

8. Intentionally Practice Hands-On Leadership

Be visible. Get out of the office and onto the floor into the work areas. Interact with your staff and team members; let them feel your presence and efforts. Take part in an interactive team-building exercise with them. When you do this the tension that might be existing within the organization might end up disappearing.

Become a mentor. Mentors guide others to success, adding value to the employee experience, and grooming internal candidates for promotion. Remember those days while you were in school, and you had this favorite teacher whose subject you liked so much and you were excelling in it without struggling or reading much?

I said in my previous book that the best CEOs of companies are usually like the best teacher you've ever had in school, college or university, they were the very teachers who used to possess the ability to make everyone in class understand the subject in simplicity, likewise, the best CEO possesses the ability to make the employees of a company understand the core business of the organization.

Since when everyone in the organization understands how the company works and generates money, they will begin to focus their efforts on areas that matters the most so that more business and cash can begin to flow into the organization. This will only happen effectively when the team leader intentionally guides and mentor his/her team players.

9. Communicate Effectively

Communicate all news–good or bad–openly, candidly, and honestly. Be sure that the employees have all of the information they need to support your organization and contribute to its future success. Communicate in all directions to all levels of the organization. Omitting people from the communication loop creates an environment of fear and distrust. Use appropriate and relevant methods of communication and make sure it is received by all staff.

Avoid using e-mail and other forms of written communication if the message is of a critical or complicated nature. Always remember that written communication is open to interpretation. Ensure that your method of communication aligns with the nature of the message. If the message mustn't be misconstrued in any way, you may need to communicate in person by holding a staff or town-hall meeting, or possibly even communicating on a one-on-one with individuals on the team.

10. Become an Agent of Change

The four major reasons that people resist change are fear of losing something they value, misunderstanding the change and what it means, believing that change is not beneficial, and low personal tolerance for change. On the other hand, you have to understand that intentional people are change agents. Embrace change; do not brace for change. Change is the only thing in life that is constant. Change is inevitable. Therefore, you must be willing to be uncomfortable at all times.

Proactively seek change. If you wait until businesses or projects are failing, then it would be too late. By not proactively changing to keep up with changes in the internal business or external environment, you have given the competition a green flag to take over your market share and put you out of business.

Involve people in the change. Whenever possible, get everyone involved in the change process. This generates buy-in and helps to alleviate some of the more negative thoughts or reactions surrounding change.

Listed Below Are Ten Ways That You Can Use to Rise Above a Crisis During a Tough Situation.

1. *Initiate Solutions*

2. *Place Demands on Your Potential*

3. *Test your creativity and that of Your Team members*

4. *Believe in Your Ability to Solve Problems*

5. *Look at What You Have, Not What You Don't*

6. *Study What You Have*

7. *Look out for the Potential of Your Resources*

8. *See Beyond the Norm*

9. *Understand the True Nature of your Resources*

10. *Place a premium on execution on everything you do*

Chapter Four

Connecting to your Intentions

I am a fan of watching documentaries for there are great lessons one learns from them. There was a documentary of ship and yacht building I once watched and from the commentator, I learned that during the early days of shipbuilding, ships were made of woods reason being its weight is low thus floats on water, unlike iron which would sink... Yet today, ships all over the world are built of iron.

As people began studying the law of flotation, it was discovered that *anything* could float if it's lighter than the mass of liquid it displaces. So today, we're able to make iron float by the very same law that makes it sink. Likewise, when you thoughtfully and intentionally put your mind on doing something that previously appeared intimidating you will end up achieving positive and breakthrough results.

Earlier on, I said that I was inspired by the flight hunger of the Wright brothers for they endeavored and ensured their flying idea ended up in the sky. They never envisaged themselves staying on the ground; rather they sweated and intentionally created wings that could take them up the sky, though they were not the only ones who dared to achieve the unthinkable and unimaginable as they did. Thomas Edison, Alexander Graham among many other inventors and innovators also purposed to intentionally connect to their field of intentions hence bringing into existence what was once thought unimaginable.

To float an idea into your reality, you must be willing to somersault the inconceivable and land on your feet, contemplating what you want instead of what you don't. Only then will you start floating your desires instead of sinking them. The law of manifestation is like the law of flotation, and you must contemplate it working for you instead of contemplating the opposite. For you to achieve this, you must be willing to connect to the world of Intentions by being Intentional with every thought and Idea God gives you and the actions you take.

Will Power and Intentional Imagination

"Nothing can withstand the power of the human will if it is willing to stake its very existence to the extent of its purpose." Benjamin Disraeli

When the human will power is activated and combined with intentional imagination, excellent results can be achieved. I have been using this power of Intentional Imagination ever since I ventured in the field of writing and publishing including in writing this book. For example, I see and imagine myself mentally as having already completed writing and publishing this book project. This concept of thinking from the end causes me to behave as if the book I am writing is already published. Your imagination allows you the fabulous luxury of thinking from the end. Nothing can stop anyone who can think from the end.

"Imagination is everything. It is the preview of life's coming attractions." Albert Einstein

Why Should You Connect to Your Intentions?

"Great Intentions become tragic action when delivered without careful thought." Michael Dooley

Leanne Watson gives us profound wisdom on why one needs to connect with their intentions.[11] If you don't choose and connect to your intentions consciously, the unconscious parts of your personality (the frightened parts) will choose your intentions for you, along with the consequences they will create for you.

It is important to connect to your intentions because **it's your intentions that set the course and determine the direction you're headed and ultimately the results you achieve**. People without clear intentions tend to roll aimlessly from one situation they don't want to another and their life becomes associated with avoidance. Whether we believe it or not, we tend to get what we think about. If you take time to assess your results, you can quite easily work out where you place the bulk of your thoughts or intentions.

---

11 **Leanne Watson:** https://www.selfgrowth.com/articles/Why_Are_Intentions_Important.html, accessed February 2021

Intentions are sometimes seen as a dogged kind of determination-forcing one to succeed at all costs by never giving up on an inner picture. Intentions activate energy in the Universe that allows the act of creation to take place. It's the process of deciding what is it that you want, getting a clear picture of it, feeling as if it's already done then detaching from the outcome. It's not so much something you do but more of the energy you are part of.

Intentions give one a sense of purpose. A person without intention is a person without a sense of purpose. When one's mind has no purpose, it tends to create pictures of what it DOESN'T WANT and then spends it's time taking evasive action. Intentions also have to be in line with your values and beliefs. When intentions are in line with your values and beliefs they flow in an almost magical way.

Anything you give calmly, certainly it will expand. So, in a relaxed and happy manner, focus your persistent and complete attention on the peaceful and powerful outcome you imagine as if that or something better is your reality. You have to remember that the universe has no distinction between imagination and reality.

The great thing about setting a powerful intention is that you can literally 'Set and Forget.' Gone is the need to stress over outcomes. Gone is the need to make a lot of difficult decisions. When you've set meaningful intentions it's easy to move from that place of being tossed around on a sea of aimlessness to a position of confident knowledge. It's so effective.

Meaningful Intentions helps one to know where he or she is coming from. When you've set meaningful intentions, you know where you're coming from. Life simply flows. The value of making that mind shift from fear and chaos to peace, knowledge of intention is a life full of purpose and synchronicity. It's a mind shift. Getting in touch with how it feels as if you already have your intention is one of the key parts of the process.

Think of a time when you were doing something you wanted to because it was important to you, you were having fun and it was unfolding according to your plan. That's the feeling surrounding an intention aligned with your highest values and beliefs. When you set Intentions based on your highest values, your life becomes full of purpose because you understand what's important to you. In conclusion, therefore; powerful intentions are shaped by knowing what's important to you and what you want to pursue and achieve in life.

The Consequences of Failing to Become Intentional Can Be Catastrophic

People all over the world recognize the name and the face of the late Steve Jobs, the visionary who co-founded Apple Computer in 1976 and led the company through the development of revolutionary products such as the Apple II computer, the Macintosh, and the iPod, a portable music player among other innovations. Not quite as well-known but still fondly remembered by computer aficionados is Apple co-founder Steve Wozniak, who developed the company's first two products (the Apple I and Apple II) but afterward held a much less visible role in the company's operations than Jobs did.[12]

12 Radido Shadrack: Homeless Money page 54, accessed March 2021

However, what many people don't know is that Apple had a third co-founder by the name of, Ronald Wayne. Wayne's name (and potential fortune) has been lost in the mists of time because he left Apple and sold off his company's interest and shares early on, thereby letting go of shares that would later be worth billions of dollars today. *Ron Wayne was the third co-founder of Apple Computer, but he soon sold his 10% share in the company for a mere $800.*

Back in the early days of Apple, when the company was a little more than an idea and a name, Steve Jobs brought in Ronald Wayne, a chief draftsman at Atari (where Jobs also worked). According to Wayne himself, he was brought into the fledgling company as a more mature voice (he was 42, while Jobs and Wozniak were in their 20's) to mediate disagreements between the other two partners:

"What must be made clear is that I was never actually involved with the soon-to-be-name computer enterprise until a modest philosophical difference arose between Jobs and Wozniak. This difference of opinion led Jobs to confide in me and seek my advice on how to resolve the issue with his friend. After reflecting on the request, I invited both men to my apartment one evening. Jobs had been sufficiently impressed by my diplomatic performance that before the evening was over; he encouraged the three of us to form a partnership. Jobs had concluded that an ideal arrangement would be that he and Wozniak should each hold a 45% stake in the new company and that I should retain 10% of the voting rights. Jobs felt that in the event of any future policy disputes, he could rely on my vote as the tiebreaker and that I'd come down on the side of rationality, rather than emotion." Ronald Wayne Said

As Steve Wozniak outlined in his 2005 mind-boggling and inspiring autobiography titled *iWoz*, Wayne quickly made himself valuable by drawing up the company's initial partnership agreement, rendering the first Apple logo, and writing the operating manual for the new company's first product, the Apple I:

"We also met with another guy from Atari, Ron Wayne, who Steve thought could be a partner. I remember meeting him for the first time and thinking, wow, this guy is amazing. He could just sit at a typewriter and type out our whole legal partnership agreement like he's a lawyer. He wasn't a lawyer, but he knew all the legal words. He was a fast talker and he seemed so smart. He was one of those people who seemed to have a quick answer for everything. He seemed to know how to do all the things we didn't.

Ron ended up playing a huge role in those very early days at Apple-this was before we had funding before we'd done much of anything. He was the third partner when I think of it. And he did a lot. He wrote and laid out the early operation manual. After all, he could type stuff. And he could draw. He was the one who did the etching of Newton under the Apple tree that was on the computer manual." However, Ron Wayne quickly developed cold feet over Job's taking out too much debt too soon, and just ten days after Apple's first partnership papers were filed, Wayne bailed on the nascent computer company:

"During the first week of my participation in the new Apple Computer Company, everything seemed to be moving along quite nicely, until some news came to light. It was positive for the company, but at the same time, disconcerting for me. Jobs, it seemed, had successfully contracted to sell 100 units of the "Apple I" computer to a retail outlet called the Byte Shop. I was told (from another source) that the Byte Shop had a terrible reputation for not paying their bills. To secure the deal, Jobs had to borrow $15,000 to acquire the components and materials to fill the order. Jobs had done exactly what he was supposed to do, but in the process, he had committed the company to a substantial obligation.

Since our enterprise was a company and not a corporation, it was an obligation that put me personally on the hook for $1,500 if the Byte Shop did indeed live up to its reputation. If worse came to worse, I had no idea where I'd come up with that amount of money. Only a few years earlier, I'd lived through my corporate failure, and spent years buying back all the stock and paying off all my creditors. There's no question that this previous experience may have clouded my reasoning at the time, but the circumstances surrounding the Byte Shop order, and the consequent monetary obligation, brought several realities immediately into sharp focus. It was those realities that led me to go back to the Santa Clara Registry Office on April 12, 1976, and remove my name from the Apple partnership."[13]

For $800, plus an additional $1,500 that Wayne received several months later when Apple was incorporated, he gave up his entire ownership interest in the company, thereby trading a 10% share of a company whose market capitalization is now close to $ 1.3 trillion. Ronald Wayne's inability to committing to his Intentions and to perceive where Apple was heading to made him sell his stake at only 2300

13 Bethania Palma, David Mikkelson: http://www.snopes.com/third-apple-cofounder, accessed February 2021

dollars. It is quite evident that he made his decision based on the previous failures and difficulties he had encountered. The past clouded his judgment, as he noted. The previous failures made him not to risk once again. He was afraid to lose all he had accumulated at the expense of the success ahead of him. He had not developed resilience capacity to push the apple dream forward as a team with the other co-founders.

He was too consumed in safeguarding what he had accumulated at the expense of what he could have benefited in future; To this day, I am pretty sure he still regrets his decision. There are so many stories out there of people who missed their breakthrough opportunities simply because they failed to become Intentional. Therefore, to avoid regretting like Wayne, purpose to become Intentional with all the decisions you take and with everything you set out to do.

Listed below are some of the simple and straight forward ways that you can practice to connect to your intentions.

1. Locate a place you can sit quietly and meditate

Find a calm, quiet spot to spend time; silence is a vital factor in the idea birthing process since the connection with thyself goes beyond the human mind. In the Execution book, I mentioned that the highest best-paid people in the world these days are great thinkers, innovators, inventors, and idea generators who possess the ability to unleash and push their ideas into execution. On the other hand, these ideas do not usually just appear into your head and mind, you have to be very intentional with the birthing and coming up with these kinds of unique and brilliant ideas.

Intentionality

The process of giving birth to ideas usually begins with the act of identifying a quiet location where you can spend quality time religiously just to birth, mold and nurture them before sharing with the rest of the world. You will come to discover that if you are a great thinker and executor your demand will always be on the rise. If you develop the ability to intentionally coming up with brilliant ideas or ways of acting on various ideas to produce positive results in the marketplace, you will never experience want or stay without a job or flow of income.

John Maxwell in his book titled thinking for a change said that he identified his best thinking places are when he spends time in his car, plane, or spa. Spending quality time in these places ignites his mind to produce creative thoughts and ideas. On the other hand, for my case, I discovered my best thinking place is when I Intentionally spends quality time in my study room, with a pen and my writing pad.

When I discovered this, I assembled some of my thinking tools, placed them in my thinking chamber, and also intentionally established Thursdays as my thinking days. On this particular day, I will spend purposely a good number of hours in my meditation place, take a clean piece of paper or my thinking note pad and write down all the ideas I intentionally decide to focus on. Embracing this habit over the past has enabled me to give birth to quality thoughts and transformative products including this book you are currently studying which was, as a result of the intentional time I have been focusing on just to think about the ideas that come into my mind and, how best to execute them.

Locating a conducive and inspiring meditation space on the other hand goes along with someone's area of passion, profession, interest, and internal stimulation. For example, a sports person, their best thinking place could be in the gym, basketball courts, football field among other related areas. Purpose therefore to locate a place that works best for you.

Idea birthing is such a precious process that needs to be accorded utmost attention, yet many people are not aware that creative ideas are the most expensive commodities in our world than all the precious stones combined.

The price tag of an idea cannot be estimated as the world marketplace values transformative ideas more than real physical assets. The beauty of an idea, therefore, is that you don't accidentally get it but you have to intentionally think your way into fishing it out and that will only happen when you identify your thinking spot and religiously spend quality time there.

2. Let Your Thoughts Go

Bring your mind to a state of inner stillness, with nothing to do or think about, even if it is just for a moment. Release any thoughts swimming around in your mind, and imagine that you are infinite intelligence, unconditional love, and all-knowing wisdom, looking out through your eyes. Sense the "I" within you that is always present, which is pure awareness.[14]

Let go of any thoughts about your outer and inner world, asking your inner self to draw you into itself. There comes a

14 Gaia Staff: https://www.gaia.com/article/how-connect-your-divine-energy-self-4-steps accessed February

time in life when you must make the difficult decision to let certain things go. Let them go. There are some opportunities, some people, some relationships, some negative associations, some attitudes, and some feelings that you have experienced that you urgently need to let go as they are hindering you from living your greatest life! they are acting as a stumbling block preventing you from entering your zone of Purpose. You're in charge of your life more so your mind. Activate your power by consciously and intentionally asking the question..." How is this serving me if I keep holding on to this limiting attitude, anger, grudge, or negative emotion?" Stop allowing these things to rob you of your peace of mind, happiness, and wellbeing or drain you financially.[15]

"Remember not the former things, nor consider the things of old. Behold, I am doing a new thing; now it springs forth, do you not perceive it? I will make a way in the wilderness and rivers in the desert. **Isaiah 43:18-19**

Let it go so that you can grow and prosper. Let it go so that you can have space for fresh creative ideas to come. Decide to release anything unbecoming of you, which does not represent your highest and best thinking. Make that decision to intentionally drop anything that does not add value to your life. This is easier said than done. It requires a decision, hard work, commitment, and being deliberate and consciously aware of your feelings. Look for ways to increase your finances, look for ways to building your capacities, look for ways to tap into your gifts, talents, and creative ideas and ways of doing business.

---

15 Radido Shadrack Homeless Money accessed February 2021

Find problems in your neighborhood, community, country, and offer solutions. That way positive return will begin to knock at your door. Don't let a temporary situation engender you to make a permanent decision about the possibilities of your future. Keep pushing forward despite the odds or how you feel at the moment. Give out but don't give up! Dare to try again but this time round in a wise manner.

Purpose from today to listen to your inner voice of purpose; silence the voices of doubt by feeding your voice of faith. Create a mental picture of success, release your excuses for playing small, and live a larger life. Use financial failures and disappointments as stepping stones to your dream; choose to be adventurous, daring, and bold, because you were truly destined for greatness. Free away the negative thoughts. The principle is that No test...no testimony and that you cannot make lemonade with sugar alone...you must have some sour lemons.

You can't learn good horsemanship by riding a tamed horse, you can't establish great and successful ventures by textbook knowledge alone, the harder the battle, the sweeter the victory on your part. You are being shaped and designed for your greatness. So let go and let God direct and take control of your path.

Look at every area of your life and ask yourself these questions: Am I on course? Am I Intentional? Am I growing mentally? Am I growing emotionally? Am I growing spiritually? Am I growing financially? Am I succeeding? If there is anything that is preventing you from pursuing your purpose, make that tough decision and let it go. Life is about surrendering and releasing. Surrendering to the higher calling of purpose and releasing all of the things, habits, and behaviors that no longer add value and meaning to you. Kick out your fears, excuses, and reasons for procrastinating. It's time to act boldly on your behalf! Refuse to play it small or safe, and refuse to chase money.

Create a bucket list of things that you have always wanted to do and then...get them out of the bucket by intentionally doing them! Visualize the places and create the experiences and memories that you want to have in this life. It's not enough to want great things in your life. It's important to EXPECT that you'll get them and act towards getting them. Want shows up in conversation, but expectation shows up in EXECUTION. Be an active force for good in your own life. Let go of your negative thoughts and let God order and direct your steps.

Be patient, continue to persist, and move in the direction of your dream. Many times, a dream has a life of its own. It will take you on a journey to build your character, your confidence, your faith, and your execution abilities. Be patient! Patience does not mean being inactive. It means positive expectation and knowledge deep down in your heart that you will be alright, the knowledge that your ideas will one-day bear fruits. Believe that things are going to work out for you, judge not according to appearances, and be patient even if you don't have money in your pocket or plan for your life.

Be patient even if you have lost your job or money. Be patient. Don't judge yourself based on what you don't have or your current situation, what you have is enough to push you ahead. Hold on to your vision, you have the power in you to resurrect your dreams and make them become a reality. Work on yourself, your attitude, and your belief system. Believe in yourself and a power greater than you.

Everyday life presents you with a full-service menu from which to choose peace or anger; sadness or joy; forgiveness or revenge; trust or suspicion; procrastination or execution; wealth or poverty. Your response to the behaviors of other people, as well as life's challenges, will determine your perception of your happiness. Happiness is a choice that you make every moment of your life. Hold happiness in your mind; pursue it with passion; show it on your face; create it within yourself, and finally, bring it out for the world to experience it in the unique spirit of you.

Talkback to yourself when fear, doubt, and negative thoughts try to stop you from believing in your power to achieve your dream. It can be difficult to be positive when things aren't going well, but you have the power to do it.

Saturate your mind with affirmations, positive audio messages, music, or anything that will inspire and lift your spirit and make you Intentional with life again. Practice filling your mind with positive thoughts, thoughts of gratitude and visions, thoughts of how your life will be different. Take charge of your life. Do not give yourself another excuse to put off making up your mind. You know in your heart of hearts that once you do that you will have to act. You owe it to the world, your family, and most importantly, to yourself to live a life of no regrets, so stop worrying about what other people will think, say or do. You only have one life to live, so live it now. Practice the skills of actively creating what you want, protecting what you value, and act decisively to change what is not working in your life.

Today, say "I do" to your vision, purpose, and dreams. Make it non-negotiable to work on your behalf and your dream every single day. This doesn't mean that you are selfish or insensitive to the people around you or other responsibilities in your life. Learning to say "No" to others and "Yes" to you... allows you to excel by setting appropriate boundaries on your time, energy, and resources. Give yourself a real gift – the freedom to be who you are and do what you were meant to do in the world. You were born to fulfill your purpose because there is greatness within you.

Reclaim your power. Get serious and chart a new course for yourself. You know that it's time to make a major shift in your life. Stop putting it off. Do it now. Follow your heart. Build a vision of a life that you love. See yourself enjoying your life and making a difference. Create a circle of friends who bring value and access to new ideas, resources, and people to your life. Listen to your call of destiny's voice then act on it.

3. Have clarity and Be Specific with your Intentions

If you aren't clear and specific about what your intentions are, how do you expect to bring them to reality? This is where a lot of people get stuck. Are you attracting what you want into your life? If not, you need to be more aware of your thoughts and tailor words more positively. For example, the words, *"I will"* are more definite than *"I hope to"* (Schwartz, 2017). The first attracts what you will do, but the second keeps you hopeful.

Know what it is that you want and make a plan to achieve it. Clear intentions lead to clear results. The Universe responds best to certainty[16] If you set goals, you're only halfway to achieving them. To truly move the needle forward in achieving those goals, it is essential to attach intentions to your goals and targets. An intention on the other hand like I had written above is simply a guiding "word" or "phrase" that you can set for your month, week, or day.

An intention's primary objective is to guide the course of your actions throughout that day. Inevitably, your intentions will align with your goals. If you, do it correctly, an intention should evoke a feeling or emotion that will align with your mind and heart. Wonder why we recommend intentions in addition to or even as a substitute to goals?

Here Are Some of The Benefits of Setting Intentions.[17]

- **Intentions have No Limits**

The wonderful thing about intentions is that you can come up with and set a new one every day through your execution planner. The possibilities of achieving all that you want are endless and when it comes to setting intentions, there's no such thing as having too many intentions. Creating a purpose for that day forces you to be present, forgiving yourself and forgetting the negative events of the past and alleviating you from any future anxieties.

16 Stefan James: https://projectlifemastery.com/setting-life-changing-intentions/ accessed February 2021
17 Silk & Sonder: https://www.silkandsonder.com/blogs/news/5-key-benefits-of-setting-intentions accessed February 2021

- ### Intentions Affect Every Aspect of Your Life

When you are clear on your intentions, you take inspired action that's in alignment with your words and truth. You also quickly manifest what you desire because you're putting out words and actions that are in alignment with the things you want to attract into your life.

Setting intentions will impact greatly on how you show up to daily activities, from your professional to physical and even mental activities among others. The same intentions will present itself in disparate areas of your life, with the power to transform your mind, body, and soul.

- ### Intentions Keep You Centered

The power of an intention-whether one or several is that they can be experienced all at once, ensuring that you feel whole. Setting intentions ensures that you don't feel that something is missing or lacking in your life since you'll be able to preview your actions at the back of your mind before physically experiencing your day. At this moment, intentions promise you feelings of presence, awareness, and fullness.

- ### Intentions Improve Your Effectiveness

By setting your intention, your subconscious mind has a magical way to ensure that opportunities to practice that intention appear in small and big ways. A positive intention leads to a positive attitude and a positive attitude on the other hand unblocks barriers and increases productivity.

- **Intentions Make You More Mindful and Productive**

You can fully immerse yourself in the present moment and not become fixated on what you don't have yet. Doing everything with intent will also help you to become more in tune with your spiritual being and this can help you approach your life more spiritually, and it will open your heart and mind to more opportunities and connections. When you commit to intentionally be doing this, it paves way for you to naturally achieve your goals and targets hence become more productive and successful in life.

Visualize Your Intentions

"Imagination is everything. It is the preview of life's coming attractions." Albert Einstein

One of the best ways to manifest your intention is to visualize and imagine yourself already having that which you desire. Psychologists and therapists highlight the importance of VAK visuals, audio, and kinesthetic modalities in shaping our minds (Nguyen, 2015). Visualization is a powerful intention-setting tool that helps us align with our purpose and create the life of our dreams. Imagination is the ability to form a mental image of something that is not perceived through the five senses. The mind can build mental scenes, objects, or events that do not exist, are not present, or have happened in the past.

The power of the mind is beyond recognition. When you start to visualize what you want in life, you will begin to see the possibility of achieving it. Imagination creates momentum and inspiration to take massive action for it inspires one internally before external efforts are taken. There is no better recipe for success than the power of intentional imagination.

The power of the human Imagination surpasses the current man-made technological innovations and inventions currently unleashed. Great inventions by men are yet to come and it is this powerful tool we all possess called the human mind that can birth such inventions. If therefore you purpose to activate your Intentional imagination power through meditation you will live the life of your dreams.

I challenge you to follow the shared thoughts discussed in this book to setting life-changing intentions for yourself and your generation. Use the power of your imagination to vividly visualize what you would like to venture and succeed in.

Allow your imagination to become a complement to your habitual action and hard work. Just like Michael Phelps says, *when you visualize, there should be no doubt at all in the outcome towards success and excellence.* Anything of value in this world requires intentional visualization.

Setting goals isn't enough. When you set intentions, it allows you to focus on and be in alignment with your values. Furthermore, it raises your emotional energy, which in turn raises your physical energy (Tabaka, 2016). If you want to master your life, commit to setting life-changing intentions and your dreams will thank you for it[18].

---

18 Stefan James: Https://Projectlifemastery.Com/Setting-Life-Changing-Intentions/ Accessed February 2021

Here is the check-list to writing your intentions

- Affirm Only What You Want
- Write as If It Is Happening Now
- Make It Believable

Be Receptive with Your Intentions

After a meditation moment, you may receive an inner message that may feel like you are giving yourself a massage, which is normal. There are people who after receiving a brilliant idea, they doubt themselves, they begin to look around for someone else to execute it on their behalf. When you begin to act like that, your idea will fly away and for sure another person who is effective with execution will act on it and reap its benefits.

Imagine if Mark Zuckerberg had doubted himself when the Facebook idea came to him? Right now, Facebook would be someone else's idea. Imagine if Bill Gates had not been receptive to the Microsoft idea? The bottom-line message here is this. When you are intentional and an idea settles at the back of your mind, you have to be receptive and plan to act on it with a sense of urgency. You don't have to spend a lot of time doing meditation; in fact, it is very effective to have frequent 2 - or 3-minutes' meditation periods during the day.

Act On Your Intentions

The end game of your imagination is the actions you take. If you spend hours doing meditation with no actions on what you were meditating and thinking about, then you are doomed to failure. This is because everything rises and falls on execution. The external expressions of people's successes that we encounter in our surroundings are as a result of the actions they committed to taking once they were done with their meditation. Therefore, you and I have to remember this *"Ideas don't make you rich, Execution of those ideas does"*

Chapter Five

The Intentional Shall Inherit the Earth

Indeed, we are living at very radical and exciting times, the business landscape and marketplace today is not as it was decades ago, governments today are not as they were back then. Competition today is much fiercer in every sphere than it was years ago, more so it has become more interesting with the emergence of technology and the Internet; the business landscape is changing with the blink of an eye.

What was once a celebrated innovative idea a few years ago is a forgotten concept today, reflecting the words of Bill Gates in his book titled *Business @ the Speed of thought* where he is captured saying *"in three years from now, every product Microsoft release will be obsolete, the only problem is whether we will make it obsolete ourselves or somebody else will. One day somebody will catch us napping. One day an eager startup will put Microsoft out of business. I just hope its fifty years from now and not two or five years"*

Intentionality

Truly this is the era of perpetual Intentionalism where only the Intentional thinkers and doers will inherit the earth by getting the job done and progressing in life. Borrowing strongly from the late writer Dr. Wayne Dyer in his book titled The Power of Intention where he wrote that a person who lives in a state of unity with the source of all life doesn't look any different from ordinary folks. These people don't wear a halo or dress in special garments that announce their godlike qualities. You will notice that they go through life as the *lucky ones* who seem to get all the breaks, but when you begin to talk to them, you will realize how distinctive they are compared to people living at ordinary levels of awareness. Spend a few moments in conversation with these people who are very deliberate and Intentional with life and you will see how unique they are.

They are usually individuals who have made themselves available for success at the all-time courtesy of their positive attitude and positive thinking coupled with leading an intentional life every moment.

One thing I am sure you will also note about these kinds of people is that it's usually very impossible to get them to be pessimistic about achieving whatever they desire in their lives. Rather than using languages that indicate that their desires may not materialize, they speak intentionally and from an Inner conviction that communicates their profound and simple understanding that the universe can provide and supply that which they ask for.

Rather than saying I don't have.... they have learned to train their minds to be asking positive questions such as *how can I have what I want* and by doing this, their minds will be intentionally running up and down looking for ways of coming up with answers.

Most of the time and even amid crisis they tend to speak to the affirmative. At times you will hear them say *I intend to achieve this or that by tomorrow afternoon* and I know I will succeed. No matter how you might attempt to dissuade them by pointing out all the reasons why their optimism ought to be curtailed, they seem blissfully blind to reality-check repercussions. It's almost as if they're in a different world, a world in which they can't hear the reasons why things won't work out.

If you engage them in conversation about this idea, they simply say something like, I refuse to think of the impossibilities since that will attract negative energy, and I'd rather embrace positivity and think about what ought to happen. It doesn't matter to them what already happened before. They don't relate to the concepts of failure or impossibility. They simply, without fanfare, are unaffected by reasons for being pessimistic. They have made themselves available for success, and they know and trust in an invisible force that's operating within them. They're so well connected to their intentions that it's as if they have a natural aura preventing anything from getting through that might weaken their connection to their power of intentions working in them. The story of Bill Gates's founder of Microsoft explains this very well.

BILL GATE'S BIG IDEA: A PERSONAL COMPUTER ON EVERY DESK AND IN EVERY HOME IN THE WORLD

Gates is one of the few founding CEOs from the technical side of the Personal Computer industry who has survived and thrived in the technology business side. He is a bona fide computer nerd. At 43, Bill Gates was the richest man in the world with an estimated net worth of $60 billion. Currently, at 64 years he is the third richest man on earth with an estimated net worth of $ 108 billion. He has headed Microsoft since he was 20 years of age; Gates' wealth is of a magnitude that is beyond the comprehension of most people and for this, he attracts both our envy and curiosity.

Bill and Paul Allen, meteoric rise to fame and fortune confirmed the creation of a new business world order: one that is dominated by a different class of entrepreneurs and business leaders. We may like to label them nerds, but they knew things that most of us knew nothing about. They created time to instinctively and intentionally learn and understand the potential of the new technology in a way that the general masses could not.

They were smart; very, very smart about stuff most people didn't understand, and it made the rest of the world uncomfortable. When it came to the future, they were able "to grasp it" much of Gates' and Allen's successes rested on their abilities to intentionally translate technical visions into market strategies and to blend creativity with technical acumen. In the end, though, what sets them apart from any other business leader in history is probably the influence that they wielded over our lives. Whereas the power of earlier tycoons was usually concentrated in one sector or industry such as manufacturing, real estate, processing, or mining, through the power of software, Microsoft extended its tentacles into every sphere of our lives.

The Intentional Shall Influence the Earth. This is seen not only through Bill Gates, but also through John D Rockefeller an American business magnate and philanthropist of founded Standard Oil, JP Morgan, Andrew Carnegie, and Steve Jobs of Apple among others. Since the early days of Microsoft, Gates set to pursue his vision of *"a computer on every desk and in every home."* Looking back now, the spread of personal computers from the office into the home seems almost inevitable. Hindsight is a wonderful thing. Foresight, however, is much more lucrative, as Gates has shown. It is important to remember, too, that the ubiquitous screens and keyboards that we all take for granted today were the stuff of science fiction just a couple of decades ago. Back in the 1960s, when futurists in America tried to predict the trends that were likely to shape society in the rest of the century, they completely missed the rise of the personal computer.

It is no coincidence either that the young Gates devoured science fiction books. The story of Gates reminds me of Henry Ford who also contributed and transformed greatly the automobile industry and Mark Elliot Zuckerberg who brought Facebook and WhatsApp to us.

In Business, the Bill Gates Way Author Des Dearlove reveals seven secrets that explain the success of Microsoft and its then remarkable CEO. Among the secrets shared are:

1. Be In the Right Place at The Right Time

It's easy to put Microsoft's success down to one extraordinary piece of good luck which was securing the contract to supply IBM the then giant company in the technology space with the operating system for its first Personal Computer. But there was more to Bill's luck than what meets the eye. Gates was able to recognize the significance of the IBM deal. He knew that it could change the history of personal computing, and worked tirelessly and intentionally for more than six months to maximize his chance of *"being lucky."* In this way, he gave luck a helping hand. When Gates was preparing to pitch for the IBM contract it is said that he told his mother that she would not see him for six months. During this time, he virtually lived at the office devoting his time entirely preparing whatever it took to win the IBM contract. He sensed how important it was and eventually won the deal. And like I wrote in the pages above; such are the characteristics of Intentional people who are so much committed to winning whatever they set out to achieve.

2. Fall In Love with The Technology and With Your Products/Services

One of the most important aspects of Microsoft's continued success was Bill Gates' technological knowledge. On many occasions, he foresaw the future direction of technology more clearly than his rivals. He was also prepared to lead the way. This is not only applicable to the technological field but also into your field of interest. For you to be effective in your marketplace, you need to possess a deeper understanding of knowledge of the product or service you are handling and knowledge of the marketplace of those products and services.

Spending quality time learning and researching about product or service in your field of interest whether it is real estate, mining, agriculture, business consultancy or any other field will give you a competitive edge and make you very effective in that field hence you will be able to command resources in your area. I have explained this in-depth in my previous book titled Execution through the Radido Triangle of Execution.[19]

Radido Triangle of Execution

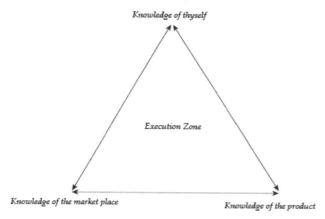

Knowledge of thyself

Execution Zone

Knowledge of the market place

Knowledge of the product

Below are some of the benefits you will experience when you have knowledge of the product or service in your venture.

Product/Service Knowledge Is Power

Mastering this power will see you closing more deals. Gates was able to close the deal with IBM among many other deals through Microsoft because he had a deeper understanding of knowledge of the product and that he could

19 Execution: Unleashing the Power to Achieve personal and corporate results page 51

foresee the future of technology. He was well acquainted with technological knowledge that he needed to thrive and take dominion of that marketplace. Therefore, for you and me to thrive in the marketplace of our venture, we ought to intentionally create time to feeding our mind with adequate knowledge of the product or service in our fields of expertise.

Product knowledge gives your prospects confidence in you. People buy people before they buy your products and services because that is how the marketplace is structured. In this journey of life, before someone transacts with you, first they will ensure that they have your confidence in what you are telling or presenting to them. And the way to have someone's confidence is by you having on your fingertip's adequate knowledge of the products or the services you are handling.

Product knowledge gives self-assurance to the person handling it. If you know more about the product than you could ever expect to use, you'll be more than prepared for any situation that comes your way. Mastering a product gives one a sense of confidence and self-assurance which in turn makes a prospect or a client believe in you, but when a client realizes that you do not have sufficient information and knowledge about the product you are selling to them closing that deal will be next to impossible.

When you gain product knowledge you will clearly understand your marketplace and competition hence standing out will be easy for you. Know your product, know also your competitor's products, and develop a competitive edge over them. For Bill Gates, his main competitor for the

IBM deal was a company called Digital Research Inc, which owned the operating system that ran the Apple II, the most successful desktop computer at that time. Sometimes your competitive edge could be on value that you offer, other times it could be on price, great customer service, or even delivering your products and services with a sense of urgency.

At a crucial stage of the IBM negotiations however, the key contact person at Digital Research, a company that was a competitor for Microsoft for the contract was away on vacation for a month. Gates, however who viewed vacations as a sign of weakness, made sure he capitalized on his competitor's absence and he eventually clinched the IBM deal, a deal which heralded a new era for Microsoft business.

Gaining product knowledge will cause you to desire learning and seeking new information to share with prospecting clients. If the product you are handling has hidden uses that you haven't yet figured out and you don't know what they are, you will find it difficult to explain to your prospect when asked hence risking losing the chances of closing the deal with the client. But if on the other hand, you have adequate knowledge and information about the product or service, your understanding and explanation about the product to a prospect will make them develop confidence in you and the product hence effective closing.

Product knowledge helps one to respond to rejections positively and with ease. The entrepreneurship journey is forever paved with rejections and objections but those equipped with confidence and knowledge of the product tend to succeed and overcome these rejections. Bill Gates faced the

Anti-trust objections but overcame them, Mark Zuckerberg co-founder of Facebook also faced the same allegations and he too overcame. This among others proves that the business landscape is paved with hurdles to be overcomed every now and then. When you gain product knowledge and receive rejections along the way, it is your passion; persistence, and positive attitude that will make you commit and eventually succeed.

1. Take No Prisoners.

Bill Gates was a fierce competitor. In everything he did, he was driven and addicted to winning. As a deal maker, this makes him an extremely tough negotiator. He made no bones about this and he was a past master at crushing competitors. He took no prisoners and markets the company's products aggressively. I have come to observe that most go-getters usually have a hunger for success and a burning desire to win at all times. It seems as if that is a common characteristic in them all. The same can be spotted in Donald Trump and the late Steve Jobs. The question, therefore, is this. Are you hungry for success?

2. Hire Very Smart People.

"High IQ people" is a Microsoft term for the very brightest people. From the start, Gates has always insisted that the company required the very best minds. He does not suffer technological fools gladly. In some quarters this has been seen as elitist and has provoked criticism. But it has several positive effects. The company can recruit many brilliant students straight from college who are attracted by the prospect of working with the very best in their fields. Hire the best of the best and you will not need to tell them what to do or bulldoze them to work. Strive to bring the best to your team and give them time and space to work; the outcome you will see is high product yield.

3. Learn To Survive.

In Microsoft, Bill Gates managed to create a voracious learning machine. Learning, he believes, is the sign of a *"smart organization,"* one that is continuously improving its internal processes; the same applies to personal development which can also be a game-changer to an individual when one commits to it. Gates mentioned that his competitors aren't so careful to improvement and from observing that, he was able to capitalize on the errors of others hence prospered. In many ways, what set him apart from other leaders in the computer industry was his focus on the business and continuous improvements. Despite his incredible success and the distractions of fame and fortune Gates remained as committed as ever.

Stick to the knitting. To date, Gates has shown himself to be remarkably resilient in a very competitive business. In large part, this is because he has been sticking to what he's good which is software.

Create a learning organization. In Microsoft, Bill Gates created what is probably one of the few genuine learning organizations in the world, the Microsoft Campus. He also succeeded in creating a continuous feedback loop. At Microsoft, he instituted feedback loops, a system where those elsewhere in the organization could provide constant feedback to their colleagues.

4. Assume The Visionary Position.

Bill Gates was a new type of business leader. Over the years, he had repeatedly shown that he was the closest thing the computer industry had to a seer. His in-depth understanding of technology and a unique way of synthesizing data gave him a special ability to spot future trends and steer Microsoft's strategy. This inspires awe among Microsoft fans and intimidated its competitors. Great lessons that we therefore need to learn here is this. What can you and I see in our future?

5. Never, Ever Take Your Eye Off the Ball.

Gates had been at the top of his profession ever since, despite his enormous wealth and achievements; he showed no signs of slowing down. He says he is driven by a "latent fear" that he might miss the next big thing. He has no intention of repeating the mistakes of other dominant computer companies such as IBM and Apple. This is usually a common characteristic of all the super successful people. They have been managing to intentionally staying hungry for success no matter how rich or wealthy they are.

Chapter Six

Intentionally Stay Broke

One of my mentors told me "When you start to increase your income, purpose to intentionally stay broke. And I mean stay broke and not staying poor." I recently started testing and putting this concept into practice and I am seeing it producing positive and tremendous results. Together with my wife we committed to saving into our sacred account, a third of what we earn which is for our future investment. It wasn't easy, we had to cut down on many things that we wanted to do with the money but for the sake of our future growth, we had to intentionally stay broke. This is the law of delayed gratification. Wikipedia defines delayed gratification as the ability to resist the temptation of an immediate reward for the sake of a much better and later reward.

We've come to observe keenly and conclude that many people these days think only in the short term, they only want what they can quickly get for the day and only go for what they can afford. Society today is operating in a season of instant gratification, an era dominated by fast-food restaurants, instant coffee shops, and instant loss of body weight without having to work hard for it. It seems as if everyone wants instant success and fails to understand that even the Roman Empire was not built on a single day but over a long time and with intentional people who had the picture of how a complete Rome would look like at the back of their minds. We are truly living in a microwave mentality era.

Never squander everything you have today at the expense of your tomorrow, never take the cheap route as you journey towards your success at the expense of the outlined route, never take the easy way out but always purpose to follow your Intentional route to your success which remains as hard work, dedication, focus, sacrifice and Intentional execution as the keys which lead to successful growth.

"The road to success is never straight, there is a curve called Failure, a loop called confusion, speed-humps called friends, red lights called Enemies, and cautions called family. But if you have a spare called determination, an engine called perseverance, insurance called faith and a driver called Vision, you shall make it to a place called success" Elekiah Manamela

Because success lies in the acquisition of knowledge, true success therefore is an ultimate demonstration of resilience and the implementation of the acquired information. Success is failure intentionally turned inside out. The path to success is not always easy. Throughout it may be slippery, you may fall easily, it might be a daunting uphill path that may tire you out and make you want to retreat, but if you are intentional and keep taking forward steps every day, you shall make it to your success. Staying broke intentionally can act as your quick breakthrough to your success.

Make some internal analysis on how moving forward you will be handling your finances, develop a list of the first things first in your vision board, and purpose to commit to sticking by them. Most people suffer financial challenges due to a lack of becoming intentional with their finances or their source of income. They end up using or enjoying today what they could have saved for a few years and have a much more reward later. Never do the mistake of eating the seeds you were supposed to plant. Your future is never ahead of you; you hold it today on your hands; purpose therefore to invest it in long term projects for there are much more rewarding benefits in that. It is never too late to begin, start now. Develop and apply this concept of staying broke all the time and in every sphere of your life and reap its rewards.

I have come to learn from myself and other people that when money, time, and other resources sit around idle, they get spent, wasted and diverted easily into unintentional projects, activities or missions that don't bring back any positive flows with them.

This state of continually staying broke has enabled us to humbly create some new revenue and stream of income adding to our mainstream which is consultancy and training through Zionpearl Business Consultants Ltd. The new stream includes House of Wealth Publishers which publishes both our writings and our various clients' work as well. Even though we are still at the early stages of our wealth creation, we believe 80 percent of wealth creation is mental while 20 percent of it is physical effort.

It will interest you to know that ever since I injected the initial capital into my first book project, I have never gone back to my pockets to raise money for subsequent reprints and for publishing the rest of the books that I have written and released. I have been saving some percentage proceeds of the books' projects into a sacred account for future investments courtesy of staying broke all the time.

In his classical masterpiece of 1926, George Clason released a book called *The Richest Man in Babylon*—one of the great success classics of all time. It's the fabled story of a man named Arkad, a simple scribe who convinces his client, a money lender, to teach him the secrets of money. In his book, George S. Clason teaches us the seven ways to curing a lean purse and among them includes:

1. **Start To Increase Your Purse by Paying Yourself First.**

The first principle the money lender taught Arkad was this: *"A part of all you earn is yours to keep."* He goes on to explain that by first putting aside at least 10% of his earnings and making that money inaccessible for expenses—Arkad would see this amount growing over time and, in turn, start earning money on its own. Over an even longer time, it would grow into a lot, because of the power of compound interest. Many people have built their fortunes by paying themselves first. It's as true and effective today as it was in 1926. Over the past years, this law had proved to be difficult and impossible for me to master and implement because every time I would pay others first and not myself, I would pay my landlord, I would pay the food vendor, I would pay the transport person, literally I would pay everyone else except myself.

When the revelation of this law shown upon my mind, I decided to keep for myself a third of what I earn. I also went ahead to keep for myself a third of the 24 hours a day life gives to me. A third of the 24 hours which is 8 hours a day, I would spend it for my personal development and growth. I would spend some hours just for meditation and thinking, other hours for studying selected personal development books, listening to selected informative YouTube teachings series such as the Men who build America as well as creating time for writing books among other personal development activities. This book you are studying is as a result of that concept as well.

Albert Einstein once said *"If you feed your mind as often as you feed your stomach, then you'll never have to worry about feeding your stomach or putting a roof over your head or clothes on your back"*

The beauty of feeding your mind first is that it will in turn give you brilliant ideas which when acted on will generate income flow that might sustain you and your family. Therefore, the first secret of fattening your purse is by coming up with a trade you can undertake, or a business you can do to generate and attract money your way. Homeless Money is attracted when you have something to offer, when you solve someone else's problems or provide a transaction of value that will bring money your way. Surely it is a law of success that unto him who keep and spend not a certain part of all his earnings, shall gold come more easily. Likewise, he whose purse is empty does gold avoid.

When I intentionally committed to setting aside a third of what I having been earning, I managed to get along just as well, I was not shorter than before, also more flows were coming my way more easily than before, this is because I had managed to create an environment where Homeless Money could find a home in what I was doing.

2. Intentionally Control Your Expenditure

One of the common challenges we all experience is that of trying to satisfy all our growing desires at a go. For a long time, I have been living on the YOLO mentality which says, you only live once and so why deny myself all that my heart desires since I didn't enjoy them while I was young? This mentality made money and all its children to be avoiding me since the little I had would get used on personal gratification as soon as it landed in my pockets.

'Necessary and unnecessary expenses' will always grow to equal your income unless you protest, and just as weeds grow in a field wherever the farmer leaves space for their roots, even so freely does desires grow in men whenever there is a possibility of their being gratified. There are limits to the distance in which someone can travel. There are limits to the extent to which you may eat. There are limits to the level of fun someone might have; controlling your expenditure, therefore, does not mean you will not have fun in life.

When the revelation of the law of controlling my expenditure began to make sense at the back of my mind, I started by tightening my expenditure belt and kept a keen eye on the income flow. I learned to draw up a budget that will support my expenditure and committed to adhering to it however much it was hard at the onset. I realized that even the so-called rich and wealthy in our society have a budget that controls their spending; this gave me assurance and confidence that I was not alone on this journey. For two consecutive months, I purposed to study thoughtfully my accustomed habits of spending and living and managed to identify spots where I was using my money unwisely.

I managed to reduce certain expenses as well as eliminating others. I also managed to introduce a simple concept of bulk shopping on some basic items. Doing so enabled us to save some money but more so we were able to save enough of our time to do other productive activities rather than queuing in a supermarket daily buying things that we could otherwise have purchased in bulk. We wrote down a list, of every item and how much it would cost and from the list we selected the necessary and also singled out those items that we could live without at the moment. Doing this enabled us to become very intentional with our spending and the way we conduct our affairs and spend our time.

Allow me therefore to introduce you to this simple and result oriented concept of controlling your expenditure and saving some of the money you earn for future investments. Purpose therefore to budget your necessary expenses and touch not the one-third that is fattening your purse. The purpose of a budget is to help your purse increase by controlling your expenses. A budget will enable you to realize your most cherished desires by defending them from your casual wishes. Therefore, keep working on your budget as you continue to adjust it and remember that in as much as you are trying to save for your investments also try on the other hand to save some amount of time just for personal meditation, Intentional thinking, and studying as well.

3. Make Your Money Multiply and Learn to Invest It.

"A man's wealth is not in the coins he carries in his purse; it is the stream of income he builds, the golden stream that continually flows into his purse and keeps it always bulging." Arkad

Money in a purse, a bank account, or a wallet is gratifying to own and satisfies a miserly soul but earns nothing. Never therefore be excited about what you have accumulated if it doesn't bring a continuous flow to you. Most people who have a pay Cheque mentality are usually excited when end month cloaks in because that is the time, they will get to earn their salaries and hold the money briefly into their hands before being used for various activities.

The wisdom I once got concerning money is that the money you have right now is not yours and the money you need, you don't have. You therefore need to come up with ways of attracting the Homeless Money that you need.

I used to experience a challenge of how to multiply my money even though I was saving a third of my income. I realized that wealth is created not just in savings only but by investing the saved amount into profitable ventures that bring positive cash flow. With the one-third you have been saving aside, try as much as you can to establish a passive stream of income where you can inject and invest those savings to generate more flows into your stream. At the beginning you might find it not easy and also the flow trickling might be small but as you progress and commit, your new stream of flow will continue to increase. Everyone on earth desires an income that flows in continuously whether you work or travel.

4. Guard Your Treasure Against Loss; Be Careful About the Investment Schemes You Get Into.

This law and principle remind me of the DECI pyramid scheme saga I once watched aired in one of our television stations where investors were lured to place their principal money into that investment scheme with the hope of it earning profits for them. In the end, they lost both the principal and the interest to be earned. The DECI saga taught me and many others the above law and that of investing in ventures that I know about. Learn to study carefully, before investing your treasure, have the assurance that your money can be safely reclaimed. Be not misled by your romantic desires to make wealth rapidly. "Before thou loan to any person, assure yourself of his/her ability to repay you and of his/her reputation of doing so[20]. And before you place an investment in any venture learn to seek more information about the danger and the possible dangers of pursuing such ventures.

George Clason says *"Almost everyone who has money is tempted by opportunities whereby it would seem that he could make large sums by its investment in most plausible projects."* He further advises that it is better to consult the wisdom of those experienced in handling money for profit than risking your money in ventures you do not know about. Therefore, never

---

20 George Clason: The Richest Man in Babylon accessed March 2021

go to a shoemaker to enquire about agricultural farming but rather to a farmer or an agricultural consultant and you will be greatly assisted.

Guard your earnings and savings against loss by investing in ventures only where your principal is safe and where you may reclaim it with ease if you desire and where you will not fail to collect a fair profit or dividend. Learn also to consult with wise men and secure the advice of those experienced in ventures you desire to undertake. Let their wisdom protect your treasure from unsafe investments.

5. Make Of Your Dwelling a Profitable Investment

Everyone desires to own a piece of property and build a home for his/her family. Recently this noble desire started to grow in us and from our earnings; we purposed to be setting aside some amount for it. Though we have not yet attained this goal of owning a house, our target as a young family is to first purchase some parcel of land in the next 5 years or less then embark on a construction journey.

"No man's family can fully enjoy life unless they have a plot of ground where his children can play safely and where his wife may raise not only blossoms but good rich herbs to feed her family. To a man's heart, it brings gladness to eat the figs from his trees and the grapes of his vines. To own his domicile and to have it a place he is proud to care of puts confidence in his heart and greater effort behind all his endeavors. Therefore, do I recommend that every man strives by whatever means to own the roof that shelters him and his family." Says Arkad[21]

---

21 George Clason: The Richest Man in Babylon page 33 accessed March 2021

6. Safeguard A Future to Come

Since human life begins from young into old age, it is advisable as George S. Clason suggests in his 6th law of increasing a lean purse that we work hard to ensure we have established a stream of income that we can depend upon even when one is not able to physically generate income due to old age. He further points out that we need to have insurance covers and policies for our various ventures and even to cover one's funeral expenses in the events he or she dies. "The man who because of his understanding of the laws of wealth acquires a growing surplus should give a keen thought to his future days. He should plan certain investments or provisions that may endure safely for many years yet will be available when the time arrives when he cannot work anymore, doing this, will not only protect himself but his generation as well.

7. Increase Your Ability to Earn (Build Your Capacity).

It is not enough to complain about tough economic times like many are doing yet you are doing nothing to change the situation. Since success and wealth creation begins from the mind, you and I need to continuously feed our minds with positive information and even acquire new skills that can enable us to increase our income or our stream of incomes. The more wisdom one has, the more he may earn. A man who seeks to learn more of his dexterity shall be richly rewarded. If he is an IT technician, he may seek to learn the methods and the tools of those most skillful in the same line. If you are a nurse, a farmer or trainer, seek to consult and exchange knowledge with others from your field, this is because keen-minded men seek greater skill that they may better serve those upon whose patronage they depend.

Therefore, I urge all who want to better their skills to be in the front rank of progress and not to stand still, lest they are left behind. If someone perfects his skills, his level of income will also increase; this is because his performance and productivity have gone up due to his ability to perform better. If you commit more interest in your work, more concentration upon your tasks, more persistence in your efforts, within a short time people will begin to admire your improved results hence your value at the workplace will go up. In conclusion to this section of staying broke, you need to pay the price for your success now so that you can pay any price tomorrow after attaining the level of success you desire. Staying broke is therefore the surest way to building your success empire.

Chapter Seven

Ten Secrets to Thriving at all Times

SECRET # 01: DEVELOP A SUCCESS GAME PLAN

An Intentional game plan is the surest pathway for accomplishing the dreams and goals of whichever magnitude you could be having. A game plan provides the road map that organizes and directs an individual or a business towards success. When priorities of a plan are unmistakably clear and specific to a team, players usually know what to focus on and, therefore, what should get their attention, resources, and follow-through.

The right priorities, combined with appropriate follow-through helps to keep the truly important things from being driven off the radar screen in the day-to-day hurly-burly of life at work or home where everything can seem urgent and important. The right priorities also can help one to rise above the constant demands that create stress and confusion.[22]

---

22 Ram Charan: Know-How: The 8 Skills That Separate People Who Perform from Those Who Don't accessed April 2021

They can enable you and me as well to provide clarity and focus for ourselves and others in our homes and organizations. Without a game plan, people are apt to try to do everything, wasting precious time and energy on things that aren't important. Therefore, train yourself to write down what you want, and then what you need to achieve what you want. Put down any chunks you need to break your goal down into (smaller wants), and also the more detailed steps along the way. Not every ambition is big enough to be broken into chunks. But whether yours is, it's certainly worth setting up some milestones.

So, for example, if you're trying to write a book, you might first need to identify the total number of pages your complete book will have and also identify the duration (in months) that you want the writing project to take and divide the two. Doing this will enable you to know the number of pages you are required to write daily for you to achieve your target. And then focus on the daily goals.

The benefit of writing things down is that you're not going to forget and on the other hand is that anything worth having is going to take some detailed thoughts, planning, preparation and visioneering. If it's not down in writing you risk leaving out something vital that might slow or even prevent you from achieving your target. None of those things is an end in itself, but without them, you won't get what you want. Milestones on the other hand are important for two reasons. One, they help you get organized so that you can launch your game plan more effectively. Secondly, they ensure you stay on track and keep pointing toward your destination.[23]

23 Richard Templar: How to Get what you want without asking, accessed February 2021

This book you are studying went through these stages I am mentioning. At first, I thought about the title, imagined how the complete book would eventually look like, ranging from the front to the back cover and the content to be written, number of pages to be written daily, and the duration of writing among others. However, the most important thing is that after all these mental reflections and imaginations, I committed to taking a pen and paper and started writing in point form the key chapter title and stories that I wanted to appear in the book as they flowed at the back of my mind. When you write something down, it ceases to become a dream or a vague wish but a solid, clear-cut out plan of action.

All those successful people you come across in your society you think they got there by accident or luck? The answer is No. They got to achieve what they currently have because of the power of a dream, a desire, a pen, and a paper, and they were not afraid of using them. They were Intentional in writing down what they wanted to achieve in life. Your success game plan should also incorporate both the long and short-term goals of where you want to be and how you want to get there.

In his book titled The Pursuit of Happiness, author and speaker Chris Gardener talks about the C5 complex of success. Allow me to take this opportunity and share the five Cs with you;

1. Be Clear

Having a plan without clear objectives and plan of action is like starting on a road trip without any idea of where you are going or how you will get there. Your plan will suffer if you try to implement your dreams without clarity. Establish clear beginning objectives and deadlines before starting your plan. While you won't be able to predict the outcome of your plan, you can clearly define the scope of your plan to give you direction on where you want to go.

2. Be Concise

Having a concise plan means being able to clearly define and express your plan of action without having to say too much. There is a lot of information around the internet that can be confusing or pulling for your attention. For most beginners, this will only confuse or frighten you, not knowing where to start.

The idea is to create a concise step-by-step actionable plan that tells you exactly what you need to do and when you need to do it. Essentially you need to map out a blueprint as if you were building a house; these instructions would guide you through what you need to do. Always be as concise as possible with your plans and remove any distractions that might be taking you away from your time in reaching your overall goals.

3. Be Compelling

When you are compelling, people are not only drawn to you, they feel compelled to be a part of what your plan is all about without even realizing it. Great plans make you feel empowered and make you believe in something greater than yourself. Stand up for what you believe in and what you are pursuing. When you are trying to do something, you are truly passionate about there is no need to worry about what others might be thinking of what you are doing.

4. Be Committed

If you want great results, you need to be committed to your plan. You will never achieve your dreams by simply being interested in the idea of getting there. You need to be committed to your actions and not just talking every day about how great you want to be and what you want to accomplish. Talking does not get the job done, the action does.

5. Be Consistent

Success does not come from what you do sometimes; it comes from what you do consistently every day. Being consistent is essential if you want to reach your dreams. It is also a real skill you must have if you want to be world-class at what you do. To be consistent means to fully dedicate yourself completely to a task, goal, or plan. It means to fully commit and stay engaged without distraction. You must consistently apply yourself to something over an extended period to reap the long-term benefits of your plan. The key here is to develop a routine that helps direct your efforts, thoughts, and actions consistently throughout the day

SECRET # 02: UNDERSTAND THAT WEALTH IS A DELIBERATE INTEND

There is nothing more common among men and women than trade, no earthly commodity more universally known, loved and pursued by many, yet more mysterious and misunderstood all over the world than money. The Americans call it a dollar, the Japanese call it Yen, the Nigerians call it Naira, the Zambians call it Kwacha and many are calling it shilling. This item seems to be the central attention of man throughout history. Many have mastered the art of chasing it, yet they have never succeeded in catching it. While few and yet wise on the other hand have also mastered the art of attracting money and making it labor for them thereby creating wealth and transforming lives.

Has it ever occurred to you that there is more money on planet earth than people? Ever since the creation of the universe, no money has left the planet earth. In fact, more money has been printed and is currently in circulation than ever before. The lovely thing about money is that it doesn't discriminate. It doesn't care what color or race you are, what class you are, what your parents did, or even who you think you are. Each day starts with a clean slate so that no matter what you did yesterday, today begins a new and you have the same rights and opportunities as everyone else to attract as much as you want based on the solutions you could be offering or the problems you could be solving.

If you therefore work hard at attracting money, you stand a better chance of becoming rich and you have to understand that money is a reward one gets after solving another person's problem. You are not given money by a committee that examines whether you deserve it or not, whether you have been good enough or not. It is a direct consequence. The amount of problem you solve, coupled with the speed at which you are intentionally solving them will determine the amount of money (reward) and the speed (flow) at which the Homeless Money will be coming your way to your bank account.

Many are the times we look at wealthy and influential people who have over the years accumulated lots of money and make all sorts of judgments about them and overlooking the fact that beneath their wealth and riches lays years and periods of sacrifices, hard work, intentional thinking and planning moments and of course the ability to take a risk and taking action on their ideas among others.

Most people are too lazy to be rich, they may say they want to be successful, but their thoughts and actions reflect otherwise. Most people don't want to do the work. Yes, they want the money but only if it comes to them by accident, luck, chance, or free tips. Then that's fantastic. They want the money that it is not tainted with their sweat, hard work, and efforts.[24]

If you are therefore serious about creating and being wealthy, you will then have to learn how the wealthy think, how they manage their time, how and where they go for networking, since there is a very big difference between the poor, the rich and the wealthy people in our society. You need to know the lingo and the language of the wealthy, even where they go for eating and the neighborhood they live in, how they work and invest.

24 Richard Templar: The Rule for Wealth, accessed March 2021

In short, you need to study money, wealth, and success if you are going to increase your prosperity. Try and get to talk to wealthy people. Ask questions. Develop a thirst for understanding and knowledge, devote to study about wealthy people, listen to their interviews, and read the books they have authored and also listen and study their autobiographies for they are always loaded with lots of insight and inspirations for success, business and life in general among others.

Please be reminded that: Poor people think, talk and discuss money all their time; Rich people think, talk and discuss material things; things like the latest car model they are driving, the houses they have bought for themselves, the number of shoes they have in their homes, the designer clothes they are wearing and other material things but; the wealthy people, on the other hand, they think, talk and discuss about ideas, they discuss opportunities and ventures they have identified and those that they are pursuing and how they are reaching out to communities impacting the lives of other people.

There is a mindset that commands wealth and one that attracts poverty, we have seen that wealth creation is a mindset, thinking that recognizes and acts on ideas. True riches and wealth creation is 80 percent mental effort and 20 percent physical effort. In conclusion, we can say that wealth creation is a mindset that needs intentional and constant improvement, exposure, and interaction with environments that stimulates it to generate creative and problem-solving thoughts and ideas that can produce a positive flow of finances upon execution.

If you have not created wealth yet, I want you to know that, it's never too late to start walking that journey. Wealth creation is not age limiting, race limiting, class limiting, or even continent limiting rather its mental limiting. You can commit to begin today and a few years down the line, you will be on your way to becoming wealthy. It all starts in our minds. It is first mental and then physical effort. It's also not too late to start investing in yourself. Grow yourself daily, become Intentional in feeding your mind with mind-opening books and related materials.

Your mind is the soil for your seeds while your seeds, on the other hand, are the ideas deposited in you by God, purpose, therefore, to intentionally cultivate your mind, as I have mentioned above, intentionally expand your capacities, and reinforce your brain power through intensive reading of books and listening to inspirational messages. Research on the books you need to study to build the capacities for where you desire to go in life. Remember that books are like fertilizers applied on a farm, for they can stimulate your mind to think creative thoughts which upon implementation will bring great benefits to you and our society.

Like I wrote in Homeless Money that Samsung, one of the largest multibillion-dollar conglomerates in the world as we currently recognize started as a small tiny seed of a grocery shop in 1938 in Daegu-Korea with only 30,000 won (Kshs 2,610), selling dried Korean fish, vegetables, and fruit to Manchuria and Beijing and now it is a multi-billion-dollar electronic giant company worth around 1.5 trillion dollars as of the writing of this book.[25]

25 Radido Shadrack: Homeless Money accessed March 2021

The founding members of Samsung throughout the years have been intentional in growing themselves through continuous personal development and learned how to effectively grow an empire from the ground up and expanding it into a global influence which they ultimately succeeded. You and I therefore have the potential of becoming the Samsung of our generation, we possess the seeds of greatness within us, and the abundance of our fruits is therefore determined by the richness of the soil upon which we plant our seed (creative ideas).

On the other hand, the richness of our soil is determined by the nutrients we pour on our soil which in this case is our creative minds. The books you and I read, the networks you and I hang around with, the friends you and I keep, and the way you and I spend our time are but some of the ways of growing ourselves to ensuring we get to our destination.

Below, I share with you a summary of the conspicuous difference of how the wealthy and the poor people think when it comes to money and success as discussed by T. Harv Eker from his book titled Secrets of the Millionaire Mind.

Poor people think MONEY is the root of all evil while the wealthy on the other hand believes POOR THINKING is the root of all evil.

You have to realize that if you view the rich and wealthy as bad and you want to accumulate wealth as they have, then you can never achieve your goals. It will impossible. How can you be something you despise? The reason why wealthy people accumulate more wealth is because they are not afraid to admit that money can solve most of their problems. The poor and poverty minded people on the other hand see money as a never-ending necessary evil that must be endured as part of life. The wealthy sees money as a great liberator and with enough of it, they can purchase financial peace of mind.

The average person has been brainwashed to believe that the rich and wealthy people use dishonesty to accumulate their success and that is why, there's a certain shame that comes along with "getting rich" in lower-income communities and because of this, most of the time you will keenly observe a person who was once living in a low-income community shifting houses and moving to a rich suburb community once he starts to accumulate wealth.

The wealthy and optimistic on the other hand know that while having money doesn't guarantee happiness, it does make your life easier, more enjoyable and gives you more options. Money is a lubricant. It enables you to "slide" through life instead of having to "scrape" by.

Money brings freedom, freedom to buy what you want, and freedom to do what you want with your time. Money allows you to enjoy the finer things in life as well as allowing you to help others have the necessities in life. Most of all, having money allows you not to have to spend your energy worrying about not having money. Thus, to change your financial narrative, you don't begin by collecting it but by feeding your mind with positive information that the wealthy feeds theirs about money and financial literacy.

Poor people think selfishness is a vice. The rich and wealthy people on the other hand think selfishness is a virtue.

The rich go out and try to make situations favorable for them; they don't try to pretend to save the world. They are go-getters, going after what they have set their minds on. The problem however is that poor-minded people view that as something negative forgetting it's that same vision that keeps them poor all the time. *"If you're not taking care of you, you might not be in a position to help anyone else since you can't give what you don't have."*

Poor people have a lottery mentality, while the Rich and Wealthy have an execution mentality.

While the masses are waiting to pick the right numbers and praying for prosperity, the great ones are solving societal problems hence making and attracting money and other opportunities for rapid growth and expansion.

"The poor and dependent minded are waiting for the government, their boss or their spouse to assist them out of their poverty situation not knowing that it's their poor level of thinking that breeds this approach to life as the clock keeps ticking away."

Poor people think the road to riches is paved with formal education while the rich and wealthy believes in acquiring specific knowledge and mastering the art of getting things done.

Many world-class performers have little formal education but have amassed great wealth through the acquisition and subsequent trade of specific knowledge and their giftedness. They have learned to master a particular skill or trade that they are using in the marketplace to generate income. Meanwhile, the masses on the other hand are convinced that master's degrees and doctorates are the way to wealth creation, mostly because they are trapped in the linear line of thought that holds them back from higher levels of consciousness...The wealthy aren't interested in the means, only the end. Their main concern is delivering results and getting things done.

Have you ever heard this advice: *"Go to school, get good grades, find a good job with a steady paycheck and work hard and then you will be successful"*? I don't know about you, but I will surely love to see someone whom this great advice worked out for them. By the way, there's nothing wrong with getting a steady paycheck, unless it interferes with your ability to earn what you're worthy of.

Poor people prefer to be paid a monthly salary or weekly wages. They prefer to trade their time for money. They need the "security" and assurance of knowing that some amount of money will be coming in at a certain time, weekly or monthly but what they don't realize is that this "security" is an illusion and it comes with a price.

The price is their wealth which they are trading in exchange with a constant monthly salary.[26] These people fail to understand that their bosses don't have a paycheck mentality nor his profit determined at the end of the month but the end of the deal. If the deal and the task is accomplished in 2 hours

26 T. Harv Eker: Secrets of the Millionaire Mind accessed March 2021

then their end month has arrived and he receives his payment but for you to have your payment, you have to wait till the end of the month.

Poor people trade their time for money, they prefer to report to work at 7:00 am and leave at 5:00 pm and get a fixed amount of salary at the end of the month. The problem with this strategy is that your time is limited thus you can't get much done. Rich people on the other hand prefers to get paid based on the results they produce, if not totally, then at least partially. Rich people usually own businesses of some form. They make their income from their profits. Some work on commission or percentages of revenue. They can also prefer to choose stock options and profit-sharing instead of higher payments.

Notice, there are no guarantees with any of the above. As stated earlier, in the financial world the rewards are usually proportionate to the risk. Rich and wealthy people believe in themselves. They believe in their value and their ability to deliver results or get things done. Poor people don't. That's why they need "security."

The poor and average people long for the good old days while the Rich and Wealthy dream of the future.

Self-made millionaires get rich because they're willing to bet on themselves, their dreams, their goals, and ideas into an unknown future. Doing this has always kept them optimistic, energetic, and intentional with everything they plan and act upon. The poor minded people on the other hand tend to believe that their best days are behind them, the days when they used to have a lot of money, bonuses, and heavy commissions and because of this, they rarely progress in life thus often struggle with depression among other diseases.

Living life with such an attitude and mentality is like driving the vehicle of their lives while focusing on the rearview mirror. I therefore want you to get it right today, that your better days are always within you, in form of dreams, visions, and ideas deposited in you by your maker thus you have to be intentional in unleashing and putting them into actions so that you and our family can enjoy life and the success that will come your way.

Poor and average people earn money doing things they don't love while the Rich and Wealthy on the other hand commit to following their passion.

One of the smartest strategies of the rich is doing what they love and find a way of getting paid for doing it. Think of Lionel Messi, Les Brown, Tyler Perry, and Steve Harvey among other gifted and successful men of influence in our current generation. What do they have in common? They are gifted and highly successful in their field of career. They are also paid for doing what is fun to them, what they enjoy doing even in the absence of pay.

On the other hand, poverty minded people take jobs they don't enjoy "because they need the money and they've been trained in school and conditioned by society to live in a linear thinking world that equates earning money with physical effort. My academic background is public health which was something I graduated with at the University but when I discovered my field of passion, I decided to trade it in exchange for what I have always been passionate about which is speaking, consulting, and publishing.

I committed to mastering the art of Public Speaking and even offered free public speaking and training sessions to various corporate organizations in the early days. Follow your passion and work it out. It's interesting to note that once you commit to following what you love doing, the universe will bend over backward to support you. Explorer W. H. Murray wrote the following words during one of his first Himalayan expeditions:

Until one is committed to passion, there is hesitancy, the chance to draw back, always ineffectiveness. Concerning all acts of initiative (and creation), there is one elementary truth, the ignorance of which kills countless ideas and splendid plans: that the moment one commits oneself providence moves in too. A whole stream of events arises from the decision, raising in one's favor all manner of unforeseen incidents, meetings, and material assistance, which no man could have dreamt would have come his way.

Poor and average people believe you have to DO something to get rich while the Rich and Wealthy believe you have to BE something to Get Rich.

While the masses are fixated on the doing for the sake of the immediate results of their actions, the wealthy on the other hand are committed to learning and growing from every experience that comes their way, whether a success or a failure knowing their true reward is becoming a human success machine that eventually produces outstanding results.

That's why people like Donald Trump can go from millionaires to nine billion dollars in debt and come back wealthier than ever and become the president of the USA. Let me remind you again that 80 percent of wealth creation is mental while 20 percent of it is physical effort, therefore pay close attention to growing your mental capacity then engage in the action part.

Poor and average people believe the markets are driven by logic and strategies while the Rich and Wealthy know it's driven by emotion and greed.

Investing successfully in the marketplace is not just about a fancy mathematics formula but understanding market trends and its operations. The rich and wealthy knows that the primary emotion that drives our financial markets is fear and greed and so they factor this understanding into all trades and trends they observe. This knowledge of human nature and its overlapping impact on trading gives them a strategic advantage in building greater wealth through leverage.

Poor and average people would rather be entertained than educated while the Rich and Wealthy prefers to be educated rather than entertained.

While the rich don't put much emphasis on furthering wealth through formal education, they appreciate the power of continuous learning even after graduating from college. Walk into a wealthy person's home and one of the first things you will not fail to see is an extensive library of books they are using to educate themselves on how to become more successful. They also have a budget for personal development where they purchase books monthly or quite often. On the other hand, the middle class reads novels; tabloids, and entertainment magazines and they wonder why they are not accumulating wealth.

Poor and average people think rich people are snobs while the Rich and Wealthy on the other hand just want to surround themselves with their like-minded.

The negative money mentality poisoning the poor and middle class is what keeps the rich hanging out with the rich because they cannot afford the messages of doom and gloom which the poor minded sing all the time. Early in my life, Mama warns me that if I keep hanging around 9 poor people, I will be the 10th one. This revelation made me desire to find out what the Rich and Wealthy feed their mind on so that I could also feed mine too and also hang around them often. It has for sure worked out for me because I ended up being infected with a thinking of their own.

Poor and average people focus on saving while the Rich and Wealthy people focus on earning and creating more income flows.

Siebold theorizes that the wealthy focus on what they will gain by taking risks, rather than how to save what they have. The masses are so focused on clipping coupons and living a frugal life that they miss out on major investment opportunities. Even amid a cash flow crisis, the rich reject the nickel and dime thinking of the masses. They are the masters of focusing their mental energy on where it belongs: on the big money. The poor minded on the other hand are living with the mentality of a penny saved is a penny earned and that is why they live their lives saving lots of penny failing to understand the lessons is not in the penny but the mind change.

Poor and average people love to be comfortable while the Rich and Wealthy find comfort in uncertainty.

For the most part, it takes guts to take the necessary risks to make it as a millionaire or billionaire; a challenge most middle-class thinkers are not comfortable living with. Physical, psychological, and emotional comfort is the primary goal of the middle-class mindset. World-class thinkers and game-changers on the other hand learn early that becoming a millionaire is not easy and the need for comfort can be devastating, therefore they have learned to become comfortable while operating in a state of ongoing uncertainty. You and I therefore need to be comfortable being uncomfortable until we achieve the intentional goals and dreams, we've set for ourselves

SECRET # 03: BE 100 PERCENT COMMITTED

The number one reason most people don't get what they want is because they don't know what they want and they are not willing to commit to getting what they want in life. If you are not totally and truly committed to creating wealth chances, are you won't. Rich people are totally clear that they want riches. They are unwavering in their desire. They are fully committed to creating wealth and success. As long as it's legal, moral, and ethical, they will do *whatever it takes* to achieve what they want. The rich and positive-minded people in our society do not send mixed messages to the universe which millions of poor and other people do.

Author T. Harv Eker reveals to us that there are three levels of so-called wanting. The first level is "I *want* to be rich or successful." The second level of wanting is "I *choose* to be rich." And finally, the third and the most important level of wanting is "I *commit* to being rich". To *commit* is "to devote oneself unreservedly." The keyword here is *unreservedly*. This means putting everything, and I mean everything, you've got into it. Most people I know who are not financially successful have limits on how much they are willing to do, how much they are willing to risk, and how much they are willing to sacrifice and put.

To be committed, you have to hold nothing back; giving 100 percent of everything you've got to achieving whatever you want. It means being willing to do whatever it takes for as long as it takes. This is the warrior's way. No excuses, no ifs, no buts, no maybes, and failure is not an option. The warrior's way is simple: "*I will be rich or I will die trying.*" "I commit to being rich." Most people would never truly commit to being rich. If you asked them, "Would you bet your life that in the next ten years you will be wealthy?" most would say, "Maybe no!" That's the difference between rich and Intentional people and the poor and unintentional ones.

In my observation and experience so far, getting rich takes focus, courage, knowledge, expertise, 100 percent of your effort, a never giving up attitude, and of course a rich mindset. You also have to believe in your heart of hearts that you can create wealth and that you deserve it.

The Inspiring Honda Story

Mr. Honda took everything he owned and invested it in a little workshop where he began to develop his concept of a piston ring. He wanted to sell his work to Toyota Corporation, and so he labored day and night, up to his elbows in grease, sleeping in the machine shop, always believing he could produce the result. He even pawned his wife's jewelry to stay in business. Finally, after he completed the piston rings and presented them to Toyota, he was told they didn't meet Toyota's standards. He was sent back to school for two years, where he heard the sarcastic laughter of his instructors and fellow students as they talked about how absurd his designs were. Rather than focusing on the pain of the experience, he decided to shift his focus on his goal. Two years later, Toyota gave Mr. Honda the contract he'd dreamt of. His passion and belief paid off because he had known what he wanted, taken action, noticed what was working, and kept on changing his approaches until he got what he wanted. Then a new problem arose.

On the other hand, the Japanese government was gearing up for war, and they refused to give him the concrete that was necessary to build his factory. Did he quit there? No. Did he focus on how unfair this was? No. Did it mean to him that his dream had died? Absolutely No. Again, he decided to utilize the experience and developed another strategy. He and his team invented a process for creating their own concrete and then built their factory. During the war, it was bombed twice, destroying major portions of the manufacturing facility. And what was Honda's response? He immediately rallied his team, and they picked up the extra gasoline cans that the U.S. fighters had discarded. He called them "gifts from President Truman" because they provided him with the raw materials, he needed for his manufacturing process materials that were unavailable at the time in Japan. Finally, after surviving all of this, an earthquake leveled his factory. Honda decided to sell his piston operation to Toyota.

Here is a man who made strong decisions to succeed. He was 100 percent committed no matter the obstacles. He had a passion for and believed in what he was doing. He had a great strategy. He took massive action. He kept changing his approaches, but still, he'd not produced the results that he was committed to. Yet he decided to persevere.

After the war, a tremendous gasoline shortage hit Japan, and Mr. Honda couldn't even drive his car to get food for his family. Finally, in desperation, he attached a small motor to his bicycle. The next thing he knew; his neighbors were asking if he could make one of his "motorized bikes" for them. One after another, they jumped on the bandwagon until he ran out of motors. He decided to build a plant that would manufacture motors for his new invention, but unfortunately, he didn't have the capital. As before, he decided to find a way out no matter what! His solution was to appeal to the 18,000 bicycle shop owners in Japan by writing them each a personal letter.

He told them how they could play a role in revitalizing Japan through the mobility that his invention could provide, and convinced 5,000 of them to advance the capital he needed. Still, his motorbike sold to only the most hard-core bicycle fans because it was too big and bulky. So, he made one final adjustment and created a much lighter, scaled-down version of his motorbike. He christened it "The Super Cub," and it became an "overnight" success, earning him the emperor's award. Later, he began to export his motorbikes to the baby boomers of Europe and the United States, following up in the seventies with the cars that have become so popular.[27]

Today, the Honda Corporation generates annual revenue of millions worth of US dollars and with over 208,399 employees all over the world, it invented the Honda Jet and is also considered one of the biggest car-making empires in Japan, outselling all but Toyota in the United States. It succeeds because one man demonstrated 100 percent commitment to his ideas and dreams which later produced life-changing results.

Giving 100 percent commitment means you are going to have to work a whole lot harder than any of your colleagues and partners. They can afford to lighten up and put their feet up a bit but for you, you can't afford to do that. To move up, you have to be 100 percent committed. You can't afford to lose sight of your long-term goal for a second. For you, there is no time off, no downtime, no lounging around time, no slipups, no mistakes, no accidental deviations from the script. You have to commit to staying committed the way Mr. Honda did. The beauty of total commitment is that you no longer have any decisions to make.

In life and business, it is almost impossible to be successful or committed if you don't have or do not set objectives of your end goal. If you don't have an objective to commit to, it is easy not to stick to it and end up where the occurrences of events take you, a bit of flotsam adrift on the

---

27 Radido Shadrack: Homeless Money, accessed 2021

eddies of life. Remember the objective that pushed Mr. Honda towards success was to develop a concept of a piston ring and sell his work to Toyota Corporation in which he did and later built the Honda Corporation Empire. What therefore is the objective that you could be willing to commit 100 percent towards?

SECRET # 04: LEARN TO SPEND LESS THAN YOU EARN

I mentioned in the pages above that for a long time I lived with the YOLO mentality which says, you only live once and so why deny myself all the good things in life? This mentality made money to elude me at all costs since it would get finished and used in personal gratification as soon as it landed in my pockets. I saw no mental and financial or investment progress in my life.

However, upon receiving the revelation of personal development, I intentionally took a drastic change and began to feed my mind and the dream I had. Every dream you have has a demand. The question that you therefore need to ask yourself is this. What is the demand of my dream? Once you've identified the demand you will need to pay the price required to achieving and fulfilling that dream otherwise you will never achieve any of them.

SECRET # 05: BECOME CREATIVE AND CULTIVATE A SKILL AND IT WILL REPAY YOU MANY TIMES

What are your skills, talents, strengths, or even weaknesses? If up to this point you do not know your area of strength or weakness, I want you to develop a personal SWOT analysis test as I broadly explained in one of my previous books titled Homeless Money highlighting both your strengths, weakness, opportunities and threats and how you can turn them into your advantage.

Try as much as you can to find out who will need and benefit from the skills you have? How do you tell the people who need these skills that you have them? What skill might you be able to master or cultivate to meet a need that's out there waiting to be met?

If you intentionally commit to developing a certain skill that the world needs, you will never experience lack. Once you can do something no one else can or something very few people can, you can pretty well name your price and cut a niche all by yourself. Believe me, it doesn't have to be a particularly difficult skill, just one that somebody else wants and is willing to pay for.

As at the writing of this book, the world is in a crisis of the COVID-19 outbreak, a viral disease that is claiming and endangering the lives of billions of people globally Kenya included. Measures put in place by the World Health Organization and governments around the world of ensuring public health standards of hand washing with soap and water or using hand sanitizers are practiced by everyone. On the other hand, an opportunity brought by this crisis is that those who have the skills of making soaps, hand sanitizers among others are truly reaping from the massive sales of these products which are currently on demand.

Intentionality

If by any chance you do not know how to manufacture a product, then you can master the art of deal-making, the art of negotiation, or the art of selling and closing. Deals are great, they can enable one to focus on their area of strength and they can make you earn money too.[28] Simple deal-making skills will save you time over and over. You therefore need to learn to be bold, to ask for more, and to trade what you have for what you want. Still, in the opportunities brought by COVID-19, you might approach a certain hand sanitizer manufacturer and negotiate a sole distributorship deal for a certain region in the marketplace.

With the art of negotiation, you have to make the other person feel they are getting as much as you are. You've got to have a lot of self-confidence and knowledge of the marketplace that you intend to sell your items among others.

Just as the art of deal-making and the art of negotiation are vital skills in business survival and life, so is the art of selling and closing. You sell products as a result of the deals you have closed. You have to sell your confidence, your trust, your ideas, and even your skills. *I often say that people buy people before buying your products and services.*

You and I have to therefore understand that selling is the bedrock upon which every fortune is built, therefore whatever you do to make yourself prosperous will in one way or another have to involve the art of selling and closing, a skill that all of us need to learn and to master. You can't make money without selling. That's a fact that every rich person knows that most of the poor people do not and that's why they are poor.

28 Richard templar: The Rule of Wealth, April accessed 2021

According to Grant Cardone, he wrote that the world is littered with the bodies of salespeople who learned how to sell but failed miserably when it came time to close the sale! Grant further wrote that there are even more people, billions, who have had great dreams only to give them up because they couldn't convince (close) others on supporting them in making those dreams become reality. Thus, the dream dies and is forgotten until someone later has the same dream, but can close others to support and accept it, and make it a reality.

Who gets the credit if we might ask you, the dreamer, or the closer? *The only real reason a person fails in life is their inability to close others on providing resources, energy, money, support, or whatever it is they need to achieve what it is they want!* It is said that 20% of people sell 80% of the world's products and services.

Everyone needs skills to survive in life. Remember Christopher Columbus convinced the Queen of Spain on funding his travels to the other side of the globe, and then was given credit for the discovery of the" New World". Inventor, Benjamin Franklin, convinced the world on electricity and because of him, we have light. JF Kennedy convinced the US population on going to the moon and thus raised the money necessary to fund space travel which ultimately achieved its mission.

Martin Luther King, Jr. convinced mankind in a very turbulent and suppressive era on the idea that all men should be treated equally, and he positively affected the world. Bill Gates also convinced the world on using a computer as a daily practice and it made him one of the richest men on the planet.

Don't forget Sir Barack Obama the former US president who convinced 60% of the US population on voting for him as President.[29]

"Learn to close, and you will never be without work, and will never be without money." Grant Cardone

In conclusion for you to effectively progress in life, you have to develop a skill that you can trade with in the marketplace.

SECRET # 06: CREATE MULTIPLE STREAMS OF INCOME

"If you have multiple streams of bills every month, you must create multiple streams of income" Ubong King

In Genesis 2:10-16, I strongly believe God is trying to teach us something here about at least having 4 streams of income. "It says *"A river watering the garden flowed from Eden; from there it was separated into four headwaters. The name of the first is the Pishon; it winds through the entire land of Havilah, where there is gold. (The gold of that land is good; aromatic resin and onyx are also there.) The name of the second river is the Gihon; it winds through the entire land of Cush. The name of the third river is the Tigris; it runs along the east side of Ashur. And the fourth river is the Euphrates. The LORD God took the man and put him in the Garden of Eden to work it and take care of it.*

I kept on wondering, if our creator, the Almighty God had at least four streams of flows into the garden how about

---

29 Closer's Survival Guide: Over 100 Ways to Ink the Deal by Grant Cardone accessed April 2021

me, his son, whom He created in his own image and likeness? Can't I establish different streams of income to flows into my bank account?

The benefits of having several streams of income is that if one stream dries up the others are able to supply and sustain the flow. The danger therefore of having and depending solely on one stream of income is that when it dries up, or affected by a crisis you might end up grounded and not being able to progress forward with life.

One of the major key differences between the poor and the wealthy that I have been able to highlight in the earlier pages is that the poor and middle-class people usually complain a lot about money and also, they try as much as they can to replicate flows of income of others while the wealthy become very creative to supplementing and adding flows of income to their existing ones. If for example, you establish a mobile money business or salon business in your area and it picks, few weeks down the line, a competitor will come and establish a replica of what you have established next to yours or directly opposite just because they are seeing yours is picking up well.

You might be wondering and asking yourself. What are the multiple streams of income otherwise known as (MSI)? MSI is not another job, multiple streams of income is not a better job, and in fact, MSI is not even a Job. MSI refers to strategies you can use to derive your income from different sources. *Having different flows of income is the quickest and easiest way to financial freedom and wealth creation.*

Money normally seems to get attracted and to flow to those who gives it the most attention and nurture it to increase. I want you to wisely understand that creating wealth especially during the early years is not just about saving alone but creating Intentional streams of income and flows that will be dripping and flowing your way.

As of the writing of this book, we are humbled to be having six different streams of income from our two different companies. That is four published books, a training company and a publishing firm. Several of our flows are drips while others flow in very well and they all need different kinds of attention and strategic positioning.

During the early years of our ventures, the major common mistake I observed several of my friends doing while running their various MSI, the mistake we also did at some point was walking away from a particular major stream of income and purely establishing another stream which is not in any way related to the earlier one. Doing this made us lose focus in the market and even building an effective and trusted brand in what we were offering became a challenge.

Strive therefore as much as you can to avoid establishing an MSI that is very different from your core business as this may lead to divided attention especially if the marketplaces of both ventures are different. For example, running a hotel business and a salon business at the same time requires different attention, skills, and marketing.

We can observe clearly from the Bible that it is one river flowing into the garden that separated into four headwaters.

The wisdom in this therefore is to first establish a strong flow of income and from it you come up with various MSI's. As I had mentioned above that MSI is not another job or even a job but a stream parallel to the main flow. And so, when you are creating your second or third stream of income, make sure they are closely connected to your main flow of income.

SECRET # 07: GET SOMEONE TO DO THE STUFF YOU CAN'T

Don't let a ten-million-dollar brain do a ten-thousand-dollar job; learn to let others do the job you can't do. This wisdom has been lingering at the back of my mind for years from the time we started our enterprise. When you pay a lot of attention trying to improve on the stuff you do not have the passion and those which you cannot do, you will end up losing quality time which you would rather have invested in your area of strength for maximum production and profitability.

Do what you are good at and get others to do the things you can't. It's that simple. Bring talented and passionate people to join your team and let them get on with the job of making your organization productive through their giftedness.

In my case, I am not good at balancing books of accounts for our ventures and so my partner does those while I focus on writing, publishing, and marketing which are my areas of strength. The beauty of delegating is that it enables one to focus on his or her areas of strength hence leading to skill and talent perfection. Richard Templar wrote in his book titled the Rule of Wealth that there are ten rules to making sure you get the right people and keep them.

Below are some of the rules you can borrow and intentionally implement to have them work positively for you.

- *Know exactly what it is you want it done and who you want to do it.*
- *Be very clear about what you want them to do for you and how much you will pay and what guidelines you will give them.*
- *Care about them for they are human.*
- *Keep them informed and motivated–Inspire loyalty.*
- *Tell them your long-term strategy–they too have a stake in your/their future.*
- *If they muck up–and they will from time to time, then correct them and move on.*
- *Praise them constantly–nothing inspires more than praise (oh, yes, and money of course).*
- *Set realistic targets but don't expect the impossible.*
- *Set a good example–be someone they can respect and look up to and set high standards and live up to them yourself.*
- *Remember you're in charge. Try as much as you can to maintain dignity, distance, and authority.*

SECRET # 08: BELIEVE IN YOURSELF AND COMMIT TO FOLLOWING YOUR INSTINCT

No man can climb beyond the limitations of his own beliefs, likewise; no person can ever believe on your behalf and implement that which you were born to do. This is because the desire and the belief have to come from within you. Your self-belief on the other hand will arise once you have painted at the back of your mind a strong picture of the result you desire to achieve. You've got to have a picture of your preferred destination at the back of your mind. This is where the wisdom of Albert Einstein comes in who was once quoted said *"Imagination is everything, it's the preview to life's coming attraction"*

Believing in yourself is therefore a choice and a decision that solely depends on you. Once you've gathered the courage to believe in yourself in everything you do, others will also believe in you and you will then discover how easy execution will become. Human belief is so strong to the extent of influencing others positively or negatively.

Intentionally work on your belief system to affect and become an inspiration to others too. Great men and women of influence in our society are those who were privileged to instinctively discover their Why for living and through that, they managed over the years to develop a strong conviction and an instinctive belief in their Why.

T.D Jake's defines instinct as being pre-wired to function in certain ways or to produce certain results. Instinct is that natural inclination towards something you love, or something you have passion for, that thing which you enjoy doing even without pay. Everyone has it and is instinctively attracted to something they strongly believe in, something that is in line with their intuition because both your life and mine advances in the direction of our instincts and if we commit to following them, they will lead us to our zone of abundance.

In the business world, it is instinct that makes certain investors to be attracted to certain ideas pitched to them for funding and partnership with the inner belief and convictions that the ideas will yield results. Your instincts will direct you to certain locations or associations that will make you connect to your destiny helper and business partners.

SECRET # 09: EXPECT THE UPS AND DOWNS, BECOME FLEXIBLE AND READY TO MOVE ON

Everything in life has its ups and downs, ins and outs, plusses and minuses. You have to know that some bits of your grand plan will go far more smoothly than you had dared to hope for, whereas others will throw up problems you simply hadn't foreseen. What I'm saying is, that's OK. It's life. You should be expecting the unexpected. Don't let the downs drag you down. Face them philosophically. Just say to yourself, "*This one too shall pass,*" and deal with it. Yes, it's a pain, but no, it doesn't have to ruin all your plans.

At the early stages while writing of this book and as I had written earlier, many nations of the world were almost at a complete lockdown, the windows of the world were shutting down, countries all over the world had imposed strict traveling measures while some had already imposed total flight ban from the affected nations because of the COVID-19 Pandemic.

Countries all over the world were and still are experiencing and feeling the economic heat of the pandemic and the rapid decision implemented. This coronavirus which is a class of respiratory disease termed COVID-19 was first detected in China quickly spread throughout Asia, Europe, the United States of America, and now Africa among other areas. The disease which was initially reported in December 2019 has infected more than 177 million people across the globe, with an account of over 3 million deaths according to WHO covid19 report[30].

According to COVID-19 business insider, UNCTAD suggests that the coronavirus is likely to cost the global economy more than USD 2 trillion, while Bloomberg suggesting a higher loss of more than USD 2.7 trillion. The total cost is yet to be quantified as the scourge is still ongoing, and there is still no clarity on effective measures to manage the economic downturn which is slowly by slowly taking the world into a 2020 recession.

Kübler-Ross elaborated to us that during a season of crisis, the five stages of loss experienced can enable someone wade through effectively and to overcome a difficult situation and move on with life.

---

30 WHO: https://covid19.who.int/, accessed April 2021

These Five Stages of Loss Include:

1. Denial

Denial is the first stage of our reactions to any form of sudden loss. It is very common for people to try and initially deny the event to subconsciously avoid sadness or the thought of pending mental struggles. Businesses and companies also experience this cycle. For example, the business owner may try to shut out reality or create an alternate reality that is preferable to his business in a difficult moment.

He may also try to convince himself that the situation is just temporary or that the crisis won't affect him or their industry. Some may even bring onboard consultants to validate the status quo rather than deal with the problem. When the first COVID-19 outbreak, case was reported, everyone was in denial including the epicenter from where it all started from in Wuhan-China. In any crisis, the first reaction is usually denial and in which people in denial often withdraws from their normal social behavior and become isolated. Denial usually does not have a set time frame, or may never be felt at all. However, it is considered the first stage of a loss.

2. Anger

The second stage of grief and loss is Anger. People that are grieving often become upset with the person or the situation which puts them in their grief state. When COVID19 reported cases started to increase in our nation, a dawn to dusk curfews in the entire Republic of Kenya was established, people were required by the government to work within the limited hours while many were forced to stay at home and to work from home. Traders, casual workers, and most people who had to get out of their homes to work in order provide for their families were very angry and upset because of the strict preventive measures put in place by the government to contain the virus.

These strict measures seriously affected both our individual and national economy while hundreds of thousands of others left stranded, depressed, and angry not knowing what to do, where to go, and which actions to take. The path of least resistance is usually characterized by anger, frustrations, and anxiety as opposed to facing the consequences of a crisis head-on.

In the case of death, the anger is often focused toward the deceased for leaving that person behind and unable to cope. In the case of COVID-19, anger was directed to those consciously spreading the virus by not adhering to self-quarantine directives yet they knew they are infected or have traveled from the infected and affected countries. Others became angry at their government because they felt the authorities could have done much more to stop the spread of the virus.

3. Bargaining

When something bad happens, have you ever caught yourself making a deal with God? Saying something like *"Please God; if you save my business through this crisis or pandemic, I will serve you with all my heart."* This is bargaining. In a way, this stage is false hope. You might falsely make yourself believe that you can avoid the grief through a type of negotiation. If you change this, I'll change that. You are so desperate to get your life back to how it was before the loss; you are willing to make a major life change in an attempt toward normalcy. Guilt is a common wingman of bargaining. This is when you endure the endless "what if" statements.

At this stage of business loss, the owners will often reach out to third parties to weather the storm and try to salvage their investments, while the vendors, on the other hand, will be asking for extended payment terms, others will negotiate with bankers for cushioning on debt covenants or to extend lines of credit and others will run to the government to save them. These are but some of the things that characterize stage 3 of loss.

4. Depression

Depression is a commonly accepted form of grief. Most people associate depression immediately with grief – as it is a "present" emotion. It represents the emptiness we feel when we are living in reality and realize the person or situation is gone or over. In this stage, you might withdraw from life, feel numb, live in a fog, and not want to get out of bed. The world might seem too much and too overwhelming for you to face. You don't want to be around others, don't feel like talking, and experience feelings of hopelessness. You might even experience suicidal thoughts, thinking "what's the point of going on?"

Oftentimes, bargaining during a crisis doesn't solve the problem mainly because of the many fears and uncertainty associated with it. Vendors are often over-extended to *their* suppliers, banks tighten up on controls, and customers are hesitant to take on new projects due to uncertainty. When the reality of the situation dawns owners may fall into despair, helplessness, and depression. After all, what's the point in soldiering on if the underlying cause is out of your control?

5. Acceptance And Moving On

The last stage of grief identified by Kübler-Ross is acceptance. In this stage, your emotions may begin to stabilize. You re-enter reality. You come to terms with the fact that the *"new"* COVID19 reality will now become your new normal. The acceptance stage is a time of adjustment and readjustment.[31] There are good days, there are bad days, and then there are good days again.

In this stage, it does not mean you'll never have another bad day coming your way, where you are uncontrollably sad. However, good days tend to outnumber the bad ones. In this stage, you may lift from your fog; you start to engage with friends again, and might even make new relationships and profits in business as time goes on.

When it comes to business, most business owners are made of pretty sturdy stuff and will not allow themselves to wallow in self-pity for long. Consequently, they will make peace with the threat and begin to develop a strategy to deal with it. How? By focusing on what's working and eliminating what isn't. Transfer resources to more profitable ventures and eliminate those products that kill margins. Hug their best customers and fire the problematic ones. Unleash the creative in their best employees and purging the ranks of bad hires.

31 Christina Gregory, PhD: https://www.psycom.net/depression.central.grief.html accessed April 2021

Crisis and catastrophe are inevitable in a business. The key is to recognize the crisis and resolve through the 5 stages of grief and quickly get back on track through effective execution.

SECRET # 10: GET THINGS DONE.... FOCUS ON INTENTIONAL EXECUTION

Execution is the final step in the pursuit of any goal, for everything rises and falls on the ability to execute and deliver results. This thing called execution is not just something that marketers and salespeople do but something that applies to every person. Nothing truly happens until you can engender the support, energy, and resources of others. As harsh as it may seem, execution is what separates those who have from those who don't.[32]

This critical and vital ability is what differentiates the dreamer from the exceptional individual who makes dreams come true. The world is filled with people who have grand dreams of new products or ideas that will change the world, but never become reality simply because the dreamer couldn't become intentional with execution. It is the ability to execute that makes a difference more than any other skill you will learn in life!

You may think this is an overstatement, but the only reason you know the names of people like Christopher Columbus, Benjamin Franklin, Abraham Lincoln, Thomas Edison, Henry Ford, JF Kennedy, Martin Luther King Jnr, Walt Disney, Mother Theresa, Bill Gates, Steve Jobs, Colonel Sanders, Oprah Winfrey, and Barack Obama among many other public figures in the world is because they were able

32 Closer's Survival Guide: Over 100 Ways to Ink the Deal by Grant Cardone accessed April 2021

to execute their ideas. They were also able to instill support in others so they could get their ideas backed with money, strategy, energy, and effort.

Execution skill is therefore needed by anyone who wants to move their ideas, dreams, products, and services into the next level of productivity. The ability to get things done is vital for anyone who wants a job or a raise or even to succeed during these tough times of COVID 19.

There is no cost to an individual or company greater than the inability to execute either on their products, services, ideas, and dreams! Grant Cardone says that the inability to get a deal done depletes an individual's belief and self-confidence. One becomes visibly demoralized and starts to give up his quest, with attention stuck on the losses and failures rather than the confidence and competence that comes from closing a deal.

The failure to close deals has devastating effects on both individuals and companies as it fuels uncertainty, insecurity, doubt, fear, loss of hope, and ultimately lost opportunities. The losses, due to the inability to execute mount up, and the expense is calculated not just financially, but emotionally as well.

The inability to execute, to finalize an agreement, to close a business deal, to engender support, is the ruin of individuals, companies, and entire industries.

Individuals, businesses, and companies fail due to their inabilities to pay undivided attention to Intentional execution, not because of a shortage of money and ideas.

Therefore, as I conclude, I would like to urge you to let your life going forward be Intentional.

Purpose To Experience:

Intentional Living

Intentional Thinking

Intentional Planning

Intentional Networking

Intentional Personal Growth

Intentional Spiritual Growth

&

Intentional Execution of your Ideas

Printed in Great Britain
by Amazon

18003496R00099